To Mr. Blakeley,
With esteem
and appreciation.

Sincerely

Ed.

The Challenge of Change

✤ ✤ ✤ ✤ ✤ ✤ ✤ ✤ ✤

The Challenge of Change

Crisis in Our Two-Party System

by EDWARD W. BROOKE

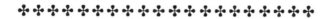

LITTLE, BROWN AND COMPANY · BOSTON · TORONTO

Published simultaneously in Canada
by Little, Brown & Company (Canada) Limited

PRINTED IN THE UNITED STATES OF AMERICA

To my father —
who cherished the
ideals of good government
and of the Republican Party

"If we could first know where we are and whither we are tending, we could better judge what to do and how to do it."

— Abraham Lincoln

❖ ❖ ❖

Introduction

A POLITICIAN writing about his party often begins by explaining how eagerly he joined it, how deeply he respects it, and how conscientiously he is working for its improvement. Let me dispense with these themes under the assumption that they are always more interesting to the teller than to the listener. Nothing is quite so tedious, self-righteous, or usually irrelevant to the fate of his party than a politician reminiscing about himself. I shall try, therefore, to confine my discussion to more significant subjects.

However, I do want to mention two or three personal matters before I begin. The first concerns my relationship to the Republican Party. As the saying goes, it has been good to me. It has given me extraordinary personal opportunities. I have enjoyed all the advantages of party support in my campaigns. I shall not have occasion in this book to describe my personal feelings of appreciation and obligation to the Grand Old Party, but I hope it will be kept in mind. It is commonplace to talk of one's debt to his party; in my case, the debt is immense.

My political career began some sixteen years ago with an unsuccessful campaign for election as representative to the lower house of the Massachusetts legislature. That defeat was repeated in 1952. Then followed in 1960 another defeat in a campaign for Massachusetts secretary of state before I was elected the Commonwealth's attorney general in 1962 and reelected in 1964. I mention this because my office is a minor one as political offices go, certainly minor as a platform for speaking out about national party issues. Republicans may be less than eager to listen to a state attorney general, and with good reason. Advice about national issues is customarily expected from elder statesmen, presidential hopefuls, and veterans of many political wars at the highest level.

I had hoped that more Republicans of national stature would publicly discuss the grave problems facing our party. But too few of our leaders have addressed themselves to our critical, underlying difficulties, and I fear we may approach the next national election as we approached the last one — woefully unprepared. Almost all Republican leaders whose approach to major issues I share have avoided the painful tasks of speaking out about our dilemmas. If we are alarmed with the course of events in recent party history and with the party's prospects, much of the blame must be placed on the reluctance to address ourselves directly to our troubles. The "good people" of the party have kept silent too long.

I shall try to outline my personal feelings in the pages that follow, feelings I might well have entertained even if the party were highly successful. But if that were the case, I would hardly have sought to publish them. If the party were even moderately successful, my thoughts about it would interest few people.

But as long as the party remains highly unsuccessful, criticism becomes not a matter of personal feeling, but the first order of party business. What might, in the flush of victory, be dismissed as individual whim or personal dissent must, in the sober quiet of repeated defeat, be considered seriously as possible sources of our troubles. Somehow we must come to grips with the attitudes of academicians, journalists, and the majority of Americans who speak and vote against us. Somehow we must face the challenge of change. It is in this spirit that I make my personal feelings public, and I urge others to do the same, no matter how severe their criticism.

No great powers of prophecy are required to predict that many Republicans will disagree with my opinions. But if this essay helps provoke discussion about the future of the Republican Party, it will have done its work. If it prompts Republicans and non-Republicans — politicians and laymen, liberals and conservatives, people mildly or passionately concerned with politics — to debate my ideas, or even reject them publicly and loudly, I shall assume it has performed a service. For we need nothing so much as we need debate. And criticism, reappraisal, *ideas*.

But there are far more compelling reasons for Republican self-appraisal than the promotion of our partisan self-interests. So marked is the present weakness of the Republican Party that the very foundation of our two-party system has become structurally undermined. When one of our major parties is dangerously weakened, its strengthening becomes a matter of national, rather than purely partisan, concern. Were it the Democratic Party that was drastically weakened, I would, I believe, feel as strongly about the need for restoring its ability to compete as I do now about reviving our own party.

At first glance one might conclude that "as the Democratic Party goes, so goes the nation." After all, it enjoys huge majorities, large enough to determine the nation's future with a freedom of action rarely available to an American party. But in a larger sense, the opposite is true: unless the imbalance of political parties is corrected, much more fundamental changes in the nation's political life will result. The country will suffer all the damage inherent in a permanent impairment of the two-party system. Therefore, I think it fair to say, "as the *Republican* Party goes in the next decade, so goes America." More than anything else, this consideration has prompted me to speak out about the party and its problems.

I am going to be critical of the Republican Party in the pages that follow, occasionally severely critical. My criticism should be preceded by a qualification. It will be directed principally to abstractions such as "the party," "the leaders of the party," "Republicanism," or "most Republicans." Everyone knows, however, that there is no such thing as "the party"; it is composed of a great number of nearly autonomous groups and individuals. And although there are, of course, "leaders of the party," they are rarely of one mind about given issues. On the contrary, there has always been considerable diversity among party leaders. Abstractions such as "the party," therefore, while convenient shorthand for "the mainstream of Republican thought and action," are bound to oversimplify specific cases.

Moreover, generalizations about the party frequently do injustice to my own segment of it. In my state of Massachusetts, for example, the Republican Party has often been the party of social reform, of pioneering legislation, of intelligent application to the problems of the present and future. It has often been the party of action and innovation, while the Democratic Party has often been mired in temporizing talk. Much of what I shall be saying about Republicans in general, therefore, will not necessarily apply to state and local Republican organizations.

Ambiguity of this sort is inherent in the nature of American parties which are essentially local rather than national. Nevertheless, some generalizations about the Republican Party as a whole have to be made, based on how *most* Republicans have reacted most often to most issues. This is the sense in which I use the terms "the party" and "the party leaders," and I hope those who think of the many exceptions to the rule will not be too disturbed by my generalizations. Describing even the major exceptions would be an endless task. Throughout, I shall try to analyze the Republican "consensus," such as it is in the nation as a whole.

When criticizing this consensus, I shall not have in mind the millions of registered Republicans who comprise the party in its largest sense. For the Republican consensus is molded by a relative handful of party leaders and officeholders — just as the Democratic consensus is molded by Democratic leaders and officeholders. Those who make pronouncements, hold press conferences, and manage affairs in our legislative bodies are the makers of what becomes known as party opinion. In the period with which I shall be concerned, the makers of Republican policy have been largely Republican members of the Congress — opposition leaders for the most part, who have acquired great seniority by virtue of continued reelection from long-standing Republican districts. My criticism is directed primarily to them. For better or worse, their statements and votes determine what is known both to historians and the public at large as the Republican position — even if they do not faithfully reflect a genuine consensus.

It is in the nature of things that this book will be considered a campaign document. And so it is, I suppose, although I am not sure at this writing whether or not I will again campaign for public office. But I am a politician, as ambitious to win elections as any other. Everything I say therefore — about politics or anything else — rightly belongs to my political record.

I hope to divorce myself here from my own political career to reflect candidly on the state of the Republican Party. Most readers will be suspicious of that, however, and perhaps they are right. Politicians rarely see conflict between the advancement of their own personal careers and the improvement of whatever party or governmental institution they are analyzing. Almost always we manage to combine the two in our thinking: "What is important," we tell ourselves, "is the development of the party." But the party development we prefer usually helps develop our personal political prospects.

It is exceedingly difficult to determine in what measure a politician is motivated by thoughts of his own career and in what measure by concern for some greater, collective good. Why does a politician write a book? To solve national problems? To satisfy his own ego? To seek a voice in the higher councils of his party? To influence public opinion? I cannot say for certain. It is easier to explain why most politicians do *not* write books. For to write a book is to put oneself forever on record. And this is something we politicians would usually rather not do.

Books by politicians are often dismissed as simply an effort to make political hay. But a writer's motivation is really irrelevant to his opinions. Of course I would prefer that this book will help, not hurt, my career. A professor writing about politics would prefer that too. Everyone is happiest when he can combine personal achievement with public service. I hope therefore that my arguments will be approved or rejected on their merits and not on speculation about the advantages or disadvantages they may bring to my personal political career.

November, 1965

Contents

[xvii]

Contents

[xviii]

The Challenge
of Change

✚✚✚✚✚✚✚✚✚

ONE

✤ ✤ ✤

Profundity of the Republican Crisis

TEN years ago, Arthur Larson, then Undersecretary of
Labor in the Cabinet of President Eisenhower, published an intriguing book entitled *A Republican Looks at
His Party*. It was an extremely optimistic, almost euphoric
analysis of American politics that predicted a lengthy era
of good times for the nation and the Republican Party.

"President Eisenhower . . ." wrote Mr. Larson, "has
operated from a conscious set of fundamental principles
. . . and . . . these principles are shared by the leaders
in his administration, by the majority of Republicans, and,
I believe, by the majority of all Americans. . . . If some
cataclysmic event does not come along which calls all bets
off, the Republicans should have a strong chance of stay-
ing in power as representatives of the great majority of
the voters. . . . Historians may someday very well conclude that the Democratic Party was the party adapted to
radical reform and free-wheeling experimentation at a
time when things were badly out of joint, while the Republican Party was the party designed to carry a more
mature America forward on a course of steady progress

[3]

and expansion, backed by the broad support of the American consensus."

No one knows what historians may someday conclude, but it hardly seems likely now that they will treat us as approvingly as Mr. Larson supposed. Whether or not his optimism about the future of the Republican Party was warranted a decade ago (and I think it was based on a faulty analysis of Republican appeal under President Eisenhower — an appeal based on admiration for the man which hardly rubbed off on the party), Republicans have little cause for self-satisfaction now. We are weak and wobbly — in a state of political exhaustion. Only once before in our history — after the debacle of 1936 — were we so overwhelmingly defeated. And we are nearly as divided and disoriented now as we were then. In terms of cohesion and esprit de corps, of the "conscious set of fundamental principles" and the "support of the American consensus" of which Mr. Larson wrote, the Republican Party has never seemed less potent. If the stale phrase "a state of crisis" has ever applied to an American political party, it applies to us now.

Statistics testifying to the present crisis of the Republican Party have been reproduced often enough in the last several years, but I wonder whether their significance has fully penetrated our collective consciousness. Republicans ought to ponder these statistics for the most obvious reasons. Yet like all politicians, we are inclined to make light of our electoral failures in order not to give the fatal appearance of discouragement. And in so doing, we are apt to mislead ourselves. Let me therefore repeat some of the salient statistics here. They require no dramatization.

In the last national election, the popular vote for the

Republican presidential candidate was thirty-eight per cent, a dismally small percentage in terms of traditional American voting habits. That figure of thirty-eight per cent is commonly cited as a symbol of Republican distress. Actually, other figures testify even more dramatically to our weakness at the national level. In Congress, for example, there are now more than two Democratic senators to every Republican (sixty-eight Democrats to thirty-two Republicans), and the ratio in the House is even worse than two-to-one (two hundred ninety-five Democrats to one hundred forty Republicans). Every aspect of our national politics, from the composition of legislative subcommittees to the quality of debate in Congress and the press, is affected by these statistics. Republicans occupy fewer than a third of our national elective offices. And as so often happens in politics when opposition strength deteriorates so drastically, our influence is in many ways less significant than our numbers might suggest.

There is a level at which effective opposition in a two-party system becomes impossible. I fear we have sunk to that level. The Democrats, surfeited with votes and legislative power, are now free to manage the affairs of state more or less as they see fit. We Republicans are more like spectators than participants.

But the national statistics, sorry as they are, fail to convey the profundity of our crisis. At state and local levels our position is even more precarious. Scores of statistics document our plight. Of fifty state governors, a mere seventeen are Republican. On the national average, Republican representation in the state legislatures has been reduced to one lawmaker in three. Republicans now con-

[5]

trol both legislative houses in a mere six states, and in areas throughout the country where, as the political commentator Richard Rovere recently put it, "Providence was believed to have ordained Republican dominance," Democrats are enjoying comfortable majorities.

Traditional Republican "dominions" in New England and the Midwest have rebelled and defected. Half of New England's Republicans voted Democratic in 1964. Maine voted for a Democratic President for the first time since 1912; Vermont became a Democratic state for the first time in history; Kansas and Indiana for the first time since 1936; Democrats control the New York State legislature for the first time in twenty-five years, and the majority in every county for the first time in history . . . and so on. With the exception of the South (and the 1964 Republican strength in the South is of questionable value and duration), Republican prestige and influence, support and spirit are grievously low. Our representation in city, county and town councils, on judges' benches and in sheriffs' and district attorneys' offices is roughly at the level to which it fell during the worst years of the Depression. Only a thorough state-by-state, county-by-county review can convey the extent of our weakness at the local level. I urge Republicans to make such a review for themselves. Here, it is enough to recognize that we are weak nationally and weaker locally.

Nor is there anything encouraging about our strength among voting "blocs" throughout the country. Among every religious, ethnic and professional group, from executives of the nation's largest corporations to unskilled and unemployed laborers, from "native" white Protestants of New England towns to ethnic minorities in major urban

[6]

centers, Republican influence and appeal has waned sharply. (The single exception again is to be found in the rural South — an exception which is more cause for alarm than for satisfaction.) Among union members and management officials, college graduates and high school dropouts, city residents and farmers, Negroes and whites, Jews, Catholics and Protestants — in all of the categories of sex, age, education, income, religion into which voting statistics are divided — support for the Republican Party has declined sharply.

Voters who had once considered themselves Republican by instinct and who remained faithful to the party from their earliest voting years are now voting Democratic. Once allegiance of this kind is shattered, it is virtually impossible to restore a sense of permanent personal identification with the party. And most disheartening of all is the Republican showing among the youngest generation of voters. In 1964 the greatest Republican weakness was in the twenty-one to thirty-nine age category: a mere thirty per cent of this group voted Republican. Moreover, there was a drastic decline in Republican affiliation among voters registering for the first time. Voting habits of a lifetime are often established in these early years — and the habits now being established bode ill for the future of the Republican Party. To an entire new generation of voters, "Republicanism" means something obscure but negative. There has been enthusiastic talk of a Republican revival among young people, but the facts are contrary: we are gaining some support loudly, but losing more of it quietly. Even among college-educated Americans who have traditionally supported Republicans, we sacrificed our majority in 1964.

[7]

One can search recent election tallies for encouraging trends, for pockets of hope, for categories of voters on which to concentrate future campaigns and appeals. Isolated victories can be discovered here and there across the country, but nothing that might honestly be called a solid structural foundation upon which to base consistent Republican majorities.

My own state of Massachusetts is occasionally cited as an encouraging example of Republican victories. Despite the Democratic landslide of 1964, as national Republican leaders like to point out, Republicans captured the three most important constitutional offices by electing a Republican governor, lieutenant governor, and attorney general. But the whole story is by no means encouraging. For the Democrats carried Massachusetts for President Lyndon B. Johnson by over a million votes, and elected a United States senator and three state constitutional officers. And as national Republican leaders fail to point out, Republicans elected but twelve of forty state senators and sixty-nine of two hundred and forty state representatives. And most tragic of all, registered Democratic voters now outnumber registered Republican voters by almost two to one in Massachusetts.

I could go on. Statistic after statistic might be quoted, one more appalling than the next, but all testifying to an ominous weakness of the party at almost every level of political activity and in almost every section of the country. The most shattering of all statistics pertains to the percentage of voters across the nation who feel a sense of personal identification with the party. In 1964 only one American voter in four considered himself a Republican.

But statistics alone never tell a complete story. They

[8]

tell nothing about discouragement and demoralization of party workers and damage to party organizations. They say nothing about the distrust harbored by Independents and Democrats, without whom very few elections can be won. Statistics only hint at the loss of confidence, among Republicans and others, in the party's ability to govern the nation.

For a political party is not merely a compilation of statistics — not merely a percentage of supporters among the voters. People can be counted; numerical strength can be measured. But the intangible assets of a party — its ideas, plans, programs; its sense of purpose and direction; its aura of confidence and demonstrated ability to direct the affairs of the nation — cannot be measured arithmetically. These intangible assets are at least as important to a party as its electoral percentage. The real test of a party measures its pulse, its cohesion, its confidence, its responses to daily political give-and-take as well as to crisis — its inner resources rather than merely its performance at the polls. And it is here that the Republican Party is weakest — weaker, I am afraid, than our numbers indicate. There is a growing sentiment in the country, strengthened by a new generation of voters who have known but a single Republican national administration, that the natural role of the Republican Party is the role of opposition. And there is a growing disenchantment about even that secondary role. Generalizations of this sort are dangerous, but I think it safe to say that millions of Americans simply do not take us seriously as a party that can be trusted to govern. "We ought to have some Republicans around," I often hear, "but not running things."

So weakened is our stature that many voters do not consider themselves faced with a genuine choice. In the voting booth the decision makes itself: Democrats appear to be the traditional governing party, the traditional winners . . . and we the traditional losers. As often happens in politics, defeat breeds defeat in a cumulative process, from election to election and from generation to generation.

I do not believe, as several political commentators appear to, that the party is in danger of withering away. American political parties have an extraordinary resilience that is woven into the very fabric of our political life. As Professor Clinton Rossiter, one of the most respected political scientists in the country, has observed, each major party is "a citadel that can withstand the impact of even the most disastrous national landslide." The Republican Party, like others in American history, has made strong recoveries in the past. Our return to at least respectable minority status after the humiliating defeat of 1936 is the most outstanding example. So great are the resources, the commitments, the forces of tradition and the means of access to the public, the strains of obstinacy and stability in the two-party system, that there is an almost built-in guarantee against total collapse. In the business and political worlds, major corporations and parties may stumble, but the odds against total bankruptcy are very great. There are plausible reasons to expect that the Republican Party may survive and to hope that someday it will again become the moving force in American politics.

It would be senseless, however, to underestimate our present weakness and difficulties. We may survive, to be sure, but we do not now possess the political resources, either in terms of ideas or organizational strength, to compete successfully in a two-party system. For those who do not accept my estimate of the seriousness of our plight, everything I shall say from this point on will sound exaggerated. If, on the other hand, there are many who do not believe our situation is grave, then in fact the situation is more grave than I had imagined. Not to be alarmed about the status of the Republican Party is, I fear, a symptom of impending rigor mortis. Or, to change the metaphor, it is a symptom of intoxication with the heady and dangerous illusion that all is well — or if not quite well, that the passage of a little more time will cure all.

TWO

✦ ✦ ✦

The 1964 Catastrophe

IN the 1964 national election the Republican Party suffered a defeat of monumental proportions far beyond
anything experienced in the normal ebb and flow of political fortunes. Not one of the party's traditional sources of
support withstood the landslide.

The causes of the 1964 catastrophe have been endlessly analyzed by political commentators, and I can add
little to the discussion beyond a simple recognition of the
obvious: Americans rejected what was inaccurately labeled
"conservatism" as resolutely as they have rejected anything in American political history. With one of the most
lopsided votes ever recorded in national politics, the electorate demonstrated that a campaign based on blanket opposition to past social achievements and future progress
can raise virtually no political capital in this era. The
1964 campaign exploded the hoary myth that a huge hid-
den conservative vote lay latent in American hearts, and
that only a candidate who offered a "choice" — the choice
of rejecting everything labeled "liberal" — could sweep
the party to victory. Our national candidates took a stand
on the great moral, legal, economic and social issues fac-

ing the nation; they assumed an outspoken position based on an ideology of ultraconservatism. And the response of the voters was even more outspoken. If there had been any doubt before, Americans demonstrated beyond any question that they will not consider the practical issues facing them in terms of ideological slogans.

The strategy of the 1964 campaign rested to a large extent on two bizarre gambles which have been called Operations "Dixie" and "Backlash." It was hoped that large numbers of Southerners motivated by anti–civil rights (or anti-Negro) sentiment would flock to the "new" Republican Party, and that a huge "backlash" movement in normally Democratic cities containing heavy concentrations of Negroes would top off the electoral bonanza. These gambles reflected shamefully on the party's moral stature. Here was the party of Abraham Lincoln, as we are proud to call it, fighting for wrong on an absolutely clear-cut ethical issue — the issue of human dignity on which the Republican Party was founded. At best, Operations "Dixie" and "Backlash" were repudiations of the Lincoln tradition. At worst, they were appeals to naked racism.

But the gambles also reflected a sophomoric approach to practical politics. They were based on a wild miscalculation of the fundamental attitudes of the American people. No principle or proposal of our 1964 presidential campaign won significant approval among the voters, for it was a campaign that appeared designed to alienate one segment of voters and then another. But of all the unorthodox strategies devised, Operations "Dixie" and "Backlash" were probably the least successful. "According to highly reliable polls made during the campaign," states the Ripon Society report, *Election 1964*, "Senator Goldwater's position on civil rights alienated more voters than did his position on any other domestic issue."

The losses suffered in November, 1964, were incalculable. The fact that Senator Goldwater carried but five Southern "hard-core" states and his own state of Arizona speaks for itself. But one significant observation ought to be mentioned as an indication of the near-total repudiation of our national candidates. It has been suggested that no matter how poorly the party fared in the nation as a whole, the electoral results offer at least one ray of hope. Now at last, according to this argument, the party accumulated the political resources for steady, solid victories in the South.

Personally, I would be deeply discouraged were the Republican Party to alter its position in order to accommodate itself to the attitudes of the traditional deep South. For that would mean a realignment of all of our thinking, a rejection of the better part of Republican ideals and tradition. Republicanism oriented toward segregation and racism would have nothing in common with the origins and history of the party. Still — the argument goes — it *would* have a permanent base of political support, and we cannot afford to ignore practical political considerations in favor of our personal penchants.

The trouble with this argument is that it ignores the inevitable changes about to overtake Southern politics. In four of the five states carried by Senator Goldwater the margin of his victories was achieved in one hundred counties where Negroes outnumber whites but cannot yet exercise their right to vote. When full voting rights are accorded Negroes in these counties, the political balance is almost certain to swing against those Republican candidates who base their appeal on a promise to outdo Democratic white segregationists. Republicanism based on segregation is anything but a permanent source of national and local party support.

The fact is that the 1964 campaign swelled Republican support in rural areas of the deep South — in just those areas where white citizens are straining to pull away from the rest of the nation on racial issues. But in the "modern" South of new industry, growing cities, and a developing tendency to accommodate itself to the rest of the nation, the 1964 campaign undermined the development of a new Republican Party. Five-sixths of the growing Republican contingent in the Texas legislature was defeated, and this symbolized the party's performance in the "new" South. In most of the South's metropolitan areas, Senator Goldwater won significantly fewer votes than did President Eisenhower in 1952 and 1956 and Vice President Nixon in 1960, sacrificing the solid Republican support that they had already built up in previous elections. In other words, Senator Goldwater's support was reduced to those areas of the old, rural (and in terms of population and influence, declining) South in which the issue of segregation is still supreme.

I do not mean to suggest that the Republican Party ought to abandon its ambition to develop a genuinely two-party South. A two-party South would be good for the South, good for the party, and good for the nation. My point is that our gains in the South not only should not, but also cannot, be achieved on the basis of racism and segregation. For us, such votes are fool's gold.

The 1964 campaign left the Republican Party in ruins,

but I do not believe the wreckage is irreparable. After all, the campaign was a "caper," a deviation from anything resembling traditional Republican values and virtues. It was the product of a coup engineered and executed by a small minority of right-wing Republicans between the elections of 1960 and 1964. They were joined by other Republicans who were earnestly seeking a conservative leader, and still others who were impressed by Senator Goldwater's hard work for the party and his personal attractiveness. Nevertheless, the minority *was* small: Senator Goldwater was the first choice as presidential candidate of only one Republican in four. And since the election the minority has shrunk further. Of those who voted for him, only twenty per cent (a mere eight per cent of the national vote) believed after the election that the Senator should be retained as party leader in 1965.

Nothing was so obvious about the campaign than the fact that Senator Goldwater represented this unrepresentative minority, not the central tradition of Republican thinking, nor the attitudes of the great mass of Republican workers and voters. The 1964 San Francisco convention was an exercise in manipulation by a zealous organization which operated with a militancy, a lack of toleration, at times a ruthlessness totally alien to Republican practices. The leaders of the organization arranged and controlled debate, so that the American public could not get a clear understanding of the issues that divided the convention. They yielded on nothing — not on the wording of the platform, not on the selection of the vice presidential candidate, not even on the phrasing of Senator Goldwater's acceptance speech, which seemed calculated to alienate all but the controlling minority. Senator

Goldwater did the opposite of what the leader of a national party should do: unite the party as it approaches a national election. (Compare this to President Eisenhower's gracious gesture in 1952 when, immediately after his nomination, he went to Senator Robert A. Taft's hotel suite to shake the Senator's hand and seek his support.) The convention was dedicated more to forcing upon the party the ideology of a narrow minority than to formulating issues and policies that might be successful during the campaign.

And this was the spirit of the election campaign too, a campaign that made loyalty to ideology the supreme virtue, regardless of the damage inflicted upon the party. Moderates were excluded from high party councils, the advice of seasoned Republican political experts was ignored, and the spirit of intraparty compromise was not so much violated as repudiated.

Extremism was not only defended as a principle of good government; it was also practiced as a tactic of intraparty politics. Portraits of Presidents Lincoln and Eisenhower were removed from the offices of the Republican National Committee. This gesture symbolized the tone of the entire 1964 campaign. This intransigence and the almost absurdly unpopular and unrealistic pronouncements of the national candidates on almost every foreign and domestic issue produced a campaign that could hardly have been less effective. We must not permit the party to be judged on the basis of this aberration.

As for reconstruction, it will require great effort. The work of restoration and rehabilitation is enormous: party organizations must be rebuilt, representative leadership reestablished, and the confidence of rank-and-file voters restored. A few Republican leaders have been quoted as predicting that the task might take a generation. It would be folly to underestimate the destruction, but surely a generation is too pessimistic a prediction. American politics, after all, are extremely volatile. Who would have predicted, after twenty years of political exile starting in 1932, that we would discover a General Eisenhower and sweep to victory in 1952?

Without question our tasks will be difficult and taxing — and without question they will be complicated by bitter intraparty struggles. But with a hard look at the mistakes of 1964 and a willingness to correct them, I do not think it unreasonable to expect that we shall soon be able to restore the party to its former strength and to return to roughly the balance of political power which existed before the 1964 tragedy.

But the balance that existed before 1964 was not good enough.

THREE

The Ominous Trend

THE decline of the Republican Party was manifest well before the 1964 presidential election. Only a party weakened, tired and confused could have succumbed to the infection we suffered in that year. Our troubles have been increasingly grave and our appeal increasingly feeble for more than a generation. One might even argue that the 1964 disaster was a blessing in disguise, for it forces us — it should force us — to face some unpleasant facts about ourselves that had not been quite unpleasant enough before to demand general attention. For decades we have been coasting downhill in a state of relative calm; 1964 was a plunge that should shock us to our senses. After this shock, we should welcome the challenge to re-examine the attitudes and policies that have failed us for a generation.

One of the most consistent facts of American political life since 1932 has been the party's relegation to minority status, a process accompanied by a slow and uneven but, in the long run, steady deterioration. By deterioration, I mean quite simply the shrinking of the party's numerical strength. According to Dr. George Gallup, the Republican Party has lost a third of its following over the past quarter of a century. While the popular vote fluctuated in accordance with the personal appeal of various candidates, popular support for Republicanism as such waned persistently. In 1940 thirty-eight of one hundred American voters considered themselves Republicans, while forty-two of one hundred thought of themselves as Democrats. From that position of near equality, Republicans were reduced in 1960 to thirty per cent of the committed voters. Professor Rossiter, writing in that year, described our dilemma neatly: "All other things being equal . . . the Republicans should lose every nationwide election. . . . They cannot register more than forty percent of American voters and cannot count on more than thirty-three percent to stand fast against temptation."

One tends to forget, in the aftermath of 1964, that even before that election, we were a distinct minority almost everywhere. Except for the eight years of President Eisenhower's administrations, Republicans have lost the presidency consistently since 1932. And the record in Congress has been worse: four years of Republican control in the last thirty-six. We won, in other words, only two congressional elections of the last eighteen. One was on President Eisenhower's coattails in the Republican "sweep" of 1952, a sweep that gave us, as the Republican historian Malcolm Moos put it, the "faltering, unworkable majority of three votes in the House, one in the Senate." The other, in 1946, was built on the shaky foundations of the accumulated frustrations of World War II. "Had enough? Vote Republican," was our slogan — and we were elected more because of public irritation over the continuation of meat rationing and other wartime restrictions than anything else.

With minor exceptions, Democrats as the majority party have made the foreign and military policy, the farm and trade policy, the space and nuclear policy of this nation during almost all of the last three decades. They have shaped civil rights and welfare laws, controlled federal appropriations and taxes, and set the tone for the great majority of legislation.

We have been in opposition so long that many of us are oriented toward securing the temporary advantages of partisan criticism, rather than developing the responsibilities necessary to govern. "With each year that passes," writes the journalist Robert J. Donovan, "fewer Republicans remain who have had important experience in handling the affairs of the United States government at home and abroad."

Nor were Republican fortunes significantly improved during the brief Eisenhower era. President Eisenhower's victories were splendid, but they were personal, not party, triumphs. They did little to rebuild lasting organizational strength within the party, and even less to win back the majority of voters. In 1956, at the very height of President Eisenhower's popularity, Dr. Gallup found that sixty-seven per cent of the American electorate identified with the Democratic Party! This indicates that there is a substantial difference between what political scientists call "Party Republicanism" and "Presidential Republicanism," and the difference is unflattering to the party.

When General Eisenhower won the presidency with

55.4 per cent of the popular vote in 1952, Republicans managed to win only a three-vote majority in the House and one vote in the Senate. But when President Harry S. Truman was elected in 1948 with only 49.9 per cent of the popular vote, Democrats won a margin of ninety seats in the House and six in the Senate. "The Republican Party is not strong enough to elect a President," Richard Nixon has perceptively observed. "We have to have a presidential candidate strong enough to get the Republican Party elected."

The statistics are dismal enough now, but they are likely to become even more so as the Supreme Court decision in *Reynolds v. Sims* (1963) is implemented during the next few years. The decision requires legislative districts in every state to be apportioned strictly on the basis of population, so that every voter has substantially equal representation. The decision is destined to have great impact on the relative strength of the two parties, and most political analysts agree that the impact is going to weigh heavily to the Democrats' further advantage. (The fact that the redistricting is going to be executed principally by Democratically controlled legislatures is sure to compound that advantage.) Much Republican strength is centered in rural areas which, in terms of population, have long been over-represented relative to cities and suburbs. Of the congressional districts that have traditionally voted Republican since 1940, less than five per cent lie in urban areas.

Things *are* as bad as they seem. Discounting the 1964 election as extraordinary, the trend is still ominous. Two Democrats to one Republican in Congress and state legislatures, four years of Republican control of Congress in the last thirty-four — these are momentous figures in a two-party system. We are not merely the minority party; we are the *perennial* minority party — and with progressively shrinking support. Contrary to what Mr. Larson predicted, it is, unfortunately, reasonable to expect continued *Democratic* majorities in the elections of 1966, 1968, and even 1970. This is what has prompted Samuel Lubell, one of America's foremost political analysts, to describe the Republican Party as "the moon in orbit around the Democratic sun."

The facts are depressing. Many Republicans prefer, quite understandably, not to think about them. After all, confidence in victory is supposed to be the first requirement of every campaign headquarters. But we cannot wish away unpleasant statistics. They exist. They accumulate. They are unarguable. They are the raw material for any reasoned analysis of our predicament and reasonable prognosis for our recovery.

Occasionally I have been advised not to mention unpleasant statistics. I have been warned that these are inappropriate times for criticism of the Republican Party, especially for criticism by a Republican. The argument has been advanced: "Don't hit a man when he's down. Be loyal to the party." Or, more explicitly: "Only a victorious party can tolerate self-criticism. If in our present difficulties we probe our own failures openly, we can only compound our discouragement and delight our enemies." More than a few Republican leaders regard self-criticism as traitorous. They feel we should save our ammunition

for the Democrats. "The Democrats, after all, are the enemy — why criticize ourselves when Democratic blunders make such juicy targets?"

But these very arguments are partially responsible
for our own more serious failures. Pretense that difficult
and disagreeable problems do not exist, unwillingness to
face them resolutely, a tendency to substitute attack on
our opponents for hard thinking about our own problems
— this state of mind has made "Republican" synonymous
with "minority" in our era. I could easily write a long essay on Democratic failures. But would that help us overcome our own Republican failures? Since the 1930's, our
emphasis on partisan attack has hurt the Democrats somewhat — but by diverting us from our own problems, it has
hurt us more. We are not fanatics; we pride ourselves on
our common sense. But clinging to a strategy long proved
inadequate has nothing in common with common sense.
Renewed party patriotism, renewed dedication to tactics
which have failed can only reduce the party's already narrow appeal. The real danger of "treason" now lurks not in
self-criticism, but in the lack of it — in a willingness to
muddle on as before, deceiving ourselves and the world
by pretending we are a potent force. If we cannot discuss
the critical problems of our own party openly and frankly,
will we be trusted to deal with the problems of the nation?

It is too much to expect that an understanding of past
mistakes will prevent a repetition of them. But surely candid analysis of earlier shortcomings promises some advantage. More than a few totally sincere and dedicated
party leaders urge us to forget the past, hold our tongues,

and build for 1968. The difficulty with this, of course, is that no one has offered a workable blueprint.

To change the metaphor, the first step in any diagnosis of illness is recognition of the symptoms. Medical analogies are often farfetched when applied to political institutions, but I think it useful to think of the party as suffering from a chronic illness.

Many Republicans will disagree with the treatment suggested here, and that is all to the good. Forthright debate about the party's future direction will attract intelligent men and women, both Republican and non-Republican. It will attract those who believe that the "democratic process is served by a rhythm which forces parties to make creative responses to the challenge of defeat."

Now is the time for the Republican Party to make such a response. I should like, therefore, to encourage an agonizing self-appraisal before we "join ranks," as the campaign slogans will have us do, and "fight for the victory of the G.O.P."

We Republicans will close ranks and fight for the victory of the G.O.P. But what are we fighting for beyond electoral victory?

✦ ✦ ✦

Political Substance

IT would be comforting to assume that accident or fate, bad luck or a bad "image" has reduced the Republican Party to chronic minority status. But these vagaries rarely produce a consistent, prolonged political phenomenon such as the thirty-five-year decline of Republican popularity. I think more fundamental causes are responsible. Our principle weakness has not been poor salesmanship, but poor programs; not a poor image so much as poor leadership. We are losing elections because Republican leaders, with too few exceptions, have been reluctant to embrace, and to mold, America's social transformations during the past three decades. They appear unprepared to guide the momentous changes now taking place. Too many Republican leaders are failing to cope with too many issues that concern too many people.

But these are abstractions. I shall try to concentrate on demonstrable circumstances and facts.

There is a long-standing tendency in the party to blame poor image-building as the principal cause of our downfall. "We must do a better job of *selling* Republicanism," say the proponents of this theory. "We've got to switch from the defensive to the offensive, employ the most sophisticated public relations techniques, get out and work to brighten the party's image." President Eisenhower gave expression to this approach when, just after the 1964 defeat, he was asked how the party ought to proceed. "We need now," he answered, "to consult among ourselves as to the methods for correcting the false image of Republicanism which far too long has confused so many of our citizens and led them to think of it as a political doctrine designed primarily for the rich and privileged."

I agree fully with President Eisenhower on the need for consulting among ourselves. But I think any purposeful consultation will end with the conclusion that "correcting the false image of Republicanism" cannot possibly be accomplished without correcting far more fundamental deficiencies. And indeed, the notion that everything can be solved by correcting our "image" — and that voters are "confused" — may distract us from understanding our underlying difficulties.

For political image is inseparable from political substance. A commercial firm can occasionally enhance the image of a product without improving its ingredients. And occasionally a skillful politician and even a skillfully led political party is capable of presenting a temporarily favorable image which is not entirely consistent with the record. But a political party cannot simply "redo" its image. A political party thrives or falters on what it says and does day in and day out in the ceaseless interaction of government, society and people. It is in the public eye or out of it continuously, in the form of speeches made and votes cast in the legislatures, public stands on pressing issues, press conferences, programs or lack of them, and reaction to the opposition's proposals. This is a party's bread and butter. This is what really determines a party's image. And there is simply too much of it that is part of the public record and accessible to the voters' daily scrutiny to change its impact with image-building campaigns designed to convince voters that the party is something different from what it is and something different from what they believe it is. I am afraid that Republicans who exhibit vast concern with image are inclined to forget that in politics, image more often than not reflects reality.

Certainly good public relations techniques are essential to successful politics. But there are limits. Cosmetics can cover blemishes and enhance one's general appearance, but public relations cosmetics cannot alter the basic shape and expression of a party. A strained effort at public relations is invariably self-defeating: it repels more potential supporters than it convinces. In an open society, a party cannot live one role with all its attitudes, values, and interests and play a different role for the public. A political party cannot act one way from the second week in November of an election year until the summer of the following election year — and hope to transform its character during the two or three supercharged months immediately prior to the next election. Such a transformation will not work because most voters' attitudes are formed over a much longer period. Most voters are too sophisticated to be "sold" by an election campaign using saturation techniques.

[28]

There is also a tendency in the party to seek recovery by seeking attractive political candidates to run on Republican tickets. "It is obvious," this argument goes, "that personality swings the balance in American politics. Find an attractive personality — a celebrity or a distinguished private citizen with political sex appeal — and the party's problems will be largely solved. After all, President Eisenhower won huge majorities despite the great preponderance of registered Democrats in the nation at large. All we really need is someone like him, and all the wringing of hands about the Republican 'dilemma' will be proved to be so much defeatist pessimism."

The argument obviously carries weight. Given the nature of American politics, the role of personality is indeed considerable. In an environment of relatively undisciplined parties composed of nearly autonomous — and sometimes antagonistic — factions, the attractive man with a flair for drama or with warmth, sincerity or father appeal often emerges on the strength of his personal image, not the importance of party platforms. Whether we like it or not, the reality of American politics is that a candidate's personality often speaks louder than his solutions to societal problems, however pressing. It would be naïve not to recognize the power of vote-by-personality.

But it is a great mistake, I think, to hope that even the most attractive political hero can alone remedy the party's underlying deterioration. We can wait for another Dwight D. Eisenhower to happen along and win the presidency for a term or two, but the fact is that all of President Eisenhower's immense political appeal did not revitalize the party at lower levels. Republican strength continued to dwindle even during his terms in office, and even more quickly thereafter. President Eisenhower was simply unable to channel his popularity into reconstruction of the national party. Nor have many attractive Republican governors and senators been able to rebuild their state Republican parties. It is often claimed that President Franklin D. Roosevelt engineered Democratic victories on the strength of his personal appeal. But actually those Democratic victories and later ones were based on an appeal to far more fundamental considerations than the personality of President Roosevelt. Obviously, individual personalities can win isolated elections and provide a flush of euphoria to party workers. But the Republican experience in the past decades has demonstrated clearly that the influence of personality is temporary and restricted.

There is still another long-standing tendency in the Republican Party: to rely upon better organization and tactics as the principal approach to recovery. "Build the party at every level," advise the proponents of this approach. "Work hard at organization, especially at the grass roots, in the geographical areas where we are weak. We can argue about principles later; now nothing is more important than solid, smooth-running party machinery which will maintain steady contact with the voters." National Chairman Ray Bliss stresses this approach to recovery: "We must place great emphasis," he says, "on year-round precinct activities in our major cities, developing a network of efficient organizations supervised by well-paid, full-time professional staffs."

Chairman Bliss is entirely correct. We do need solid, smooth-running party machinery, especially in major cities, where Republican organizations often hardly function at all. We need more active precinct, ward and district committees — hard-working committees that spend their time in meaningful political activity: recruiting, registering and fund-raising. However, this need only reflects more fundamental needs. Successful party committees cannot materialize out of thin air in the precincts, wards and districts where they are needed most. Their development is integrally linked to the party's substantive appeal in those areas — to the party's attitudes toward the problems of those areas. Or to put it conversely, one can imagine a Republican organization on every block of every city — and none of them able to engineer a conversion to Republicanism if the party's policies remain unsatisfactory.

I do not mean to imply that organization and tactics are irrelevant or unimportant. On the contrary, they are essential to successful politics. Nor do I mean to imply that there is something lacking in the spirit and dedication of Republican Party workers. No one who has campaigned on a Republican ticket could make such an implication. I know hundreds of Republican Party workers who labor literally to exhaustion, giving their time, their energy and their money (and contrary to common myths, it is often money they can little afford to give) in order to elect Republican candidates and strengthen the party organization. Unfortunately, however, they are often handicapped by a failure on the part of Republican leaders to provide them with attractive substantive issues with which to work. When party workers ring doorbells and shake hands, when they arrange meetings and distribute literature, they must have something to "sell." Good organization and good tactics by themselves are not enough.

A party's organization and tactics, like its image, cannot be divorced from its substance.

I am not convinced that Republican troubles are fundamentally those of organization techniques and campaign tactics. However, I am convinced that we need to improve our performance in those areas. The countless little pre-election meetings where we are welcomed ardently by our supporters and we preach to the converted are necessary to build Republican morale. But in the face of a two-to-one Democratic majority, Republican candidates and Republican organizations must concentrate on independent and Democratic voters. I question the inordinate emphasis placed upon "strengthening party unity," and reciting and recounting the evils of the Democrats — a kind of G.O.P. super-patriotism which often serves (though most often inadequately) as a substitute for substantive, constructive policy. And I decry the atmosphere of intense partisanship which tends to turn us inward upon ourselves, instead of outward where the critical voters are. There *is* much to criticize in our allotment of time, our sense of proportion, our plan of attack, and above all, that slightly distant, suspicious attitude toward non-Republicans which makes so many of them suspicious of *us*.

I think much could be achieved by some considered changes in Republican tactics. Consider, for example, our failure to take advantage of the opportunities offered by the growth of American suburbs. Since World War II, there has been a huge migration from city to suburb, and a strong vote in the suburbs is now crucial to political success. Many of the new suburbanites are offspring of immigrants who had traditionally voted Democratic in the city. As new home-owners in the suburbs, however, many of them have a strong propensity to change their allegiance to the Republican Party. But they need some sincere encouragement — a welcome from the local Republican organization, an honest effort to recruit them. They should receive a letter of welcome upon their arrival and subsequent visits to discuss their problems and the problems of the community. But instead of grasping this opportunity for Republican recruitment, some of our suburban organizations retreat to the company of the old "in-groups," erecting real and psychological barriers to prospective new members in order to protect "seniority rights." Consequently, many potential Republican voters are alienated, and too many suburbs have become Democratic as the cities have long been.

In other words, too many Republican Party organizations seem to be pervaded by a distant, inaccessible attitude which sours the relationship between Republican "regulars" and the great masses of voters. The entire Republican Party suffers when any Republican organization fails to welcome people of various social and religious backgrounds. But we all suffer more whenever a condition exists that might be called "inbreeding" — a condition in which party workers appear more concerned with maintaining control of their organizations than with broadening the base of the party, and more fearful of losing that control than losing elections.

We suffer too wherever a similar attitude prevails in the selection of our candidates for public office — wherever the interests of the "ingroups" take precedence over the interests of the party as a whole. Wherever the opposite is true — wherever candidates are selected on their mer-

[33]

its, regardless of their social and ethnic background —
the party benefits. In the last decade in Massachusetts, for
example, John Volpe, the son of an Italian immigrant, was
three times nominated by the Republican Party for the
governership, and twice elected. George Fingold, a Jew,
was three times elected a Republican attorney general,
and then nominated by the Republican Party for the gov-
ernorship, an office which he doubtless would have won
had he not suffered an untimely death. And I, a Negro,
have been three times nominated for statewide office by
the Republican Party, and elected twice.

Selection of candidates is one of the most important
functions of a party at any level. Like the practice of politics itself, it requires a delicate balance of science and art.
Candidates must be matched to the office and the issues.
They must be matched against their opponents and their
chances to *win.* But sometimes seniority and inertia determine the selection: stalwarts from the "ingroups" are
chosen because they are "deserving" — not so much deserving to win, but, it is thought, deserving to run. I have
attended too many conferences in which party leaders
have said, "Let X run — he deserves a shot at that office"
— without any consideration of X's "electability." When
"outside" talent *is* recruited, most often it is done among
businessmen, under the notion that business success is
somehow the most valid test of political success. Certainly
both undertakings require talent, but the talent required
is not necessarily the same. "Has he ever met a payroll?"
is not the first question to be asked in selecting a candidate. It is far more important to ask, "Has the prospective
candidate ever demonstrated any ability to cope with po-

litical issues and understand social forces, any capabilities working in civic groups, any popular appeal?"

Where the Republican Party organizations stifle the initiative of young people, the consequences are particularly unfortunate. Too often, young people with talents and energy and with new ideas are frustrated. Their enthusiasm and drive to improve the party are often throttled. In some instances, they are not excluded — but neither are they encouraged. And where young people with fresh ideas are discouraged to the point of joining the Democratic Party, we lose priceless political capital.

We lose political capital too wherever a parallel phenomenon exists in our Young Republican Clubs. These clubs sometimes reflect and other times even magnify the attitudes of their parent bodies. They can, and many do, contribute to the party's success. But others are not what they ought to be: a cross section of American youth. Those clubs exhibit a certain exclusiveness in their social and economic composition. Although it may not be deliberate, although the leaders of the clubs may sincerely wish it otherwise, many young people feel they are unwanted. Youth of Irish, Negro, Italian, Jewish, Slavic, Mediterranean and other "foreign" ancestry are often unaware of the existence of Young Republican Clubs. And when they do learn of them — I have heard this complaint from many young people of "minority" groups — they tend to dismiss them as social cliques reserved for a distinct and limited group of friends.

Wherever this occurs, wherever Young Republicans fail to recruit the broad masses of young Americans, they are hurting our cause. Although they should be building the party's future, in fact they are undermining it by allowing "Republicanism" to be associated with "reserved" and "unwelcome."

Not all of our organizational and tactical problems derive from a single source. But I believe there is a central deficiency underlying our approach to tactics and organization, and central to most of our shortcomings. Our campaigns suffer when we fail to go where the greatest number of voters are. I discussed this problem with "Mr. Speaker," Representative Joseph W. Martin of Massachusetts, on a plane returning to Boston from the 1960 Republican National Convention in Chicago. Mr. Martin told me a story that his mother had told him as a boy and he had never forgotten. And it is a story that Republicans should never forget. "Joe," Mrs. Martin said, "when you want to fill your pail with huckleberries, go where the huckleberries grow."

But too many Republican candidates do not go where the huckleberries grow. It is common knowledge that Republican support is weakest in the lower economic groups, where the most votes lie. The late V. O. Key, Jr., perhaps the most respected political scientist of his generation, has documented that common knowledge exhaustively with public opinion statistics. "The most common image of [American] parties," he wrote, "relates them to the causes of occupational and economic interests. Business and professional people have tended by large majorities to picture the Republican Party as the party that best serves their interests. At the opposite end of the occupational hierarchy, unskilled workers picture the Democratic Party as the agent of their interests. . . . As the people who make up a randomly chosen national sample ruminate in response to open-ended questions on what they like and dislike about the major political parties, they make five or six times as many references to group affiliations favorable to the Democratic party as to the Republican party."

All this is well known. Yet many Republicans still talk abstractly about "winning new voters" without coming to grips with the fact that the new voters we are talking about are in the lower income groups. And there is a similar unwillingness to recognize that we must win new votes specifically among minority groups. In 1960 and 1964 we lost some eighty per cent of the Jewish vote, seventy-five per cent of the Catholic vote, and from seventy-five to ninety-five per cent of the Negro vote. Our support among Irish-Americans, Italian-Americans, Polish-Americans is slim. Our problem was neatly described by former National Chairman Leonard Hall in 1965 in the Long Island newspaper *Newsday*. "The other day I attended a meeting of Republican congressional leaders and others who want to help in the Republican congressional campaign of 1966. Someone said, 'What's wrong with us?' 'Look around the table,' I said. Here we were, a white Anglo-Saxon Protestant group. There was not a Jewish man there. There was not a Polish-American. There was not an Italian-American. There was not a Negro. The person next to me said, 'Len, I think there's one Catholic.' "

Most minority groups vote Democratic largely by default: Democrats have not won them so much as we have lost them. In fact we all but exiled them, including those minority groups such as the Negroes who were once staunch Republicans. Geographically, too, much of our

[37]

campaigning is not directed to the areas where it is most needed. It is well known that Republican support is weakest in the cities. The deeper one advances into city centers, the sharper the plunge in Republican votes. The greater the problems of people caught in crowded urban centers — and the less able these people to deal individually with their problems — the smaller the influence of Republicanism. More and more, urban Americans have adopted Democrats as their champions. To urban Americans, we appear to have turned our backs on the cities. And in response they have turned their backs on us.

Hundreds of statistics testify to the weakness of Republican support in America's cities. Less than a fifth of the nation's cities of over thirty thousand population are served by Republican mayors, and in the larger cities the imbalance is even greater. Less than a tenth of the congressional districts of America's largest cities are represented by Republicans. Whichever statistics one chooses to cite, they demonstrate beyond question that the big cities, the middle-sized cities, and even the little cities with few exceptions are overwhelmingly Democratic. In Samuel Lubell's phrase, America's urban millions stand "like a human wall between the Republicans and their past dominance." Yet our campaign efforts are not primarily concentrated in the cities, where they are most needed. We are apt to lose contact with large segments of the population we consider instinctively hostile. Of course, it is precisely these "hostile" voters to whom we must appeal or forever remain the minority party.

But this is no mere mistake in campaign technique. Many Republican candidates tend to avoid many of the more populous groups among the voting public because they have too little to offer them. We are (again, I am speaking in general) out of touch with their problems, needs and outlook. There is a failure of communication between us; we do not speak the same language. And so we stick to our own and withdraw from real, as opposed to last-minute, preelection competition for their votes.

The most brilliant campaigning — the slickest salesmanship and the fanciest oratorical wrapping — cannot put us in touch with the problems, needs and outlook of that majority of voters. The majority has been rejecting what we say (or do not say, which in politics is the same thing) — not just the way we say it.

It is all too easy to assume that we can rehabilitate the party simply by improving our tactics, image and organization. But tactics, image and organization are only the outward reflections of a party's outlook and philosophy — of its substance. It is to that substance that we must turn our attention.

✣ ✣ ✣

Analysis of Criticism

W HY are we the minority party? Let us begin the disagreeable task of analysis not with theory or history,
but with the attitudes of some voters who criticize us.
This may seem an odd place for a politician to begin because politicians have a way of avoiding people who criticize them. In the Republican Party there is some tendency
to reject criticism as evidence of bad faith or evil intent. I
was surprised and disappointed to hear President Eisenhower respond in this manner at the 1964 National Convention in San Francisco. To the accompaniment of wild
cheers, President Eisenhower advised us to ignore the
criticism of the press. "Let us particularly scorn the divisive efforts of those outside our family," he said, "including sensation-seeking columnists and commentators . . .
because, my friends, I assure you that these are people
who couldn't care less about the good of the party."

Nothing President Eisenhower said at the convention
was more warmly received; and nothing, I am afraid, was
less felicitous. This statement, so uncharacteristic of him,
reflects a certain insularity that encourages us to believe
we can "go it alone" because the press, the political com-

mentators and the political scientists are wrong, and we alone are right. Political parties cannot flourish when they harbor an innate suspicion of the press and of the popular attitude which the press reflects. The press is not a natural enemy bent on distorting Republican positions and misinforming the public about what Republican officeholders do. Whenever Republicans assume a defensive stance toward the press, they do the party a greater disservice than anything the press could possibly do. The same, of course, applies to the Democrats. For surely President Truman's loss of temper with members of the press hurt the Democratic Party also.

People do not vote for us for a hundred different reasons, good and bad, real and imagined, logical and irrational. Family prejudices, historical accidents, even the color of a candidate's eyes determine the voting habits of some Americans more than a sensible calculation of their own and the national interest. Yet I think it fair to speak of a central theme which runs through the adverse comments about the Republican Party.

We are known by tens of millions of American voters as a minority party that in fact represents a minority: the rich and well-born. It is said that we cater to the secure and vested interests of America's upper classes and that for less fortunate groups we offer little besides messages of inspiration. It is charged that we have no constructive programs, no creative thinking — that we do not attempt to understand the working man's problems. And it is argued that this is not accidental, because we are not eager to recruit the working man into the party. In a word, we are said to be the party of the privileged.

[41]

"You talk a lot about individual rights and opportunity for all and the American Way of Life," a working man rather typical of these millions told me last summer in Fall River, Massachusetts. "But to tell you the truth, I don't think the Republican leaders *know* too much about our way of life. What do you think individualism and opportunity mean for us — that we should run right out and buy factories? We want to better our lives as working families. Now, I don't want to hurt your feelings, but I think the Republican Party is cold and calculating. Why are you against Medicare? Why are you against social security? Why are you always *against* everything? The Republicans have been against every good idea for people like me since I can remember. You don't seem to like people or to care about people. You've got some good brains on your side — but no heart."

I smiled. I had heard those comments many times before. "Yes," I answered, "but can you imagine a body with a heart and no head? What the country needs now, sir, is a good head. We need people who can think — who can solve the problems of this age."

And I *do* think the country needs a head, an extremely able head. But the man was right: the country also needs a heart. No body can survive without both.

For some time now, we have been known as a party with little heart — a cold party lacking humanity. Whether we care to admit it or not, we are thought of as a party which by nature is anti-labor, anti-old age, anti-minority groups, anti-social progress, anti-youth, anti-underprivileged — anti-everything humane. It is said that we marshal all of our intelligence and resources to devise a dozen high-sounding reasons for saying "no," and that we are so concerned with protecting the status quo for privileged groups that we thwart the legitimate aspirations of others. The majority of the nation feels that we are not genuinely interested in their welfare.

To put it bluntly, we are known by most citizens who vote against us as a party so concerned with price that we neglect to appraise the merchandise. And the merchandise in politics is people.

"Not so," we protest. The people who reason this way are simply misguided — fooled by Democratic demagoguery and promises. If we spent as much time as the Democrats on propaganda instead of on sound ideas and sound government — and if we were willing to squander as much of the taxpayers' money as they — we might convince the majority of Americans that we are better equipped to promote the general welfare in its largest sense, and better equipped to offer them more genuine progress in the long run. We do not thwart legitimate aspirations. On the contrary, the very essence of Republicanism is to encourage them.

And it *is* not so. Surely we are not guilty to the degree our critics charge. Surely our unfortunate image among many voters is, at least partially, the product of unskilled campaign techniques, amateurish public relations, and popular myths assiduously cultivated by the Democrats. Surely we are not the party of everything anti-humane. Nor are we always against everything. We are not against civil rights and social security; many of us were not against Medicare. All of us sincerely believe that Republicanism, given the chance, would provide opportunity and justice for all. And we can deliver a dozen arguments and cite a hundred facts to prove it. We can outline our posi-

[43]

tions, define our principles, quote from our platforms. We can list a splendid record of humane Republican achievements. And we can explain at great length why millions of citizens *do* vote for Republicans.

But it is always easy to convince oneself of the rightness of his own cause. In politics, however, what one believes about himself is of secondary importance. We must convince the voters, especially the skeptical and critical voters. It is a grave delusion to assume that our critics are victims of demagoguery. They are making a point by voting against us. Are we willing to listen?

Their point appears to be simple: we are the party of the privileged, of big business and other vested interests; therefore we are indifferent or hostile to the aspirations of people whose interests are neither vested nor secure. But I think this interpretation is oversimplified and too easily refuted.

In America, it need not be a liability to be known as the party of business, even big business. The word "business" like the word "big" has always had a respected ring in our vocabulary. More than any other country in the world, America is a business country, business-minded and business-oriented. Business has helped create an economy whose productivity and efficiency stagger the imagination, and whose continued efficient operation and expansion are essential to the welfare of every citizen. "Businessman" is a respected title; "businesslike" is a complimentary adjective; and business itself is a synonym for the serious pursuit of serious interests. Business is vital to all aspects of our lives, and its exceptional successes have made it an object of near universal admiration. American business is an institution of extraordinary folk genius, and it is recognized as such, consciously or intuitively, by almost all voting Americans.

We need not be defensive, therefore, about being called the party of business. Properly interpreted, that role can be an asset, rather than a liability. Properly guided, the party of business could be the party of the entire nation. After all, Democratic Presidents, the current one more and more successfully — than most, court big business when they can. And they are not ashamed to do so. Association and cooperation with business have not hurt the Democrats. And if our working relationships with other groups are sound, an excellent relationship with business will not hurt us. Of course the Republican Party is for business. That must not mean, however, that we become dominated by business to the detriment of other interests — that by being for business we are against other groups.

Nor is the contention that we are "upper-class" a fundamental source of our troubles. By itself, "upper-classness" need not be a serious stigma. There is simply not enough class antagonism in America to make significant political capital out of this kind of resentment. Like most peoples (perhaps more than most peoples because we tend to de-emphasize the importance of classes), Americans are quite willing to choose leaders from the upper classes. Some of our most popular politicians have been millionaires — and conspicuous among them have been *Democratic* millionaires. Like "big business," "upper-class" can be an asset. It can mean — it should mean — competence, excellence, intellectual integrity, and other qualities necessary for success. Americans are far more inclined to admire achievement and to strive to emulate it than to resent it.

I think the disapproval inherent in the unfavorable image of the Republican Party does not concern who we are so much as what we have done — and more important, what we have not done. We have failed, the voters are saying, to deal with their problems *as they see them*. We have been unwilling to discharge the functions of government in our complex society. We have not been successful in dealing with the real issues of the past three or four decades. These are the damaging charges.

And here, I think, the charges correspond to a certain reality. The sad truth is that since 1930 it has been the Democratic Party that has conceived and executed most of the great programs of social and economic reform which have proved essential to the well-being of a complex industrialized and urbanized society. In the areas of social security, wage and hour laws, fiscal countermeasures against depression and recession, support for beleaguered farmers and banks, unemployment compensation and programs for full employment, improvement of health and education, of beautification and conservation — in short, in dozens of areas essential to the harmony and humaneness of an industrialized society and the protection of individuals against its hazards — it has been the Democrats who sought solutions, proposed and enacted legislation (and became the majority party) while Republicans generally procrastinated, protesting "no."

It was not so much that our solutions to the great problems of our age were wrong; our great failure has been that we have often had no solutions at all. Since the middle third of the century when the character of American society began to change more and more rapidly in the direction of an enlightened, responsible capitalism seek-

[46]

ing to guarantee a distribution of its vast benefits for all citizens, Republicans have been on the defensive. We have been reduced to the role of opposition, often sullen opposition, intensified by the lack of alternative suggestions of our own. We have criticized Democratic administrations. We have protested about the welfare state. We have warned about creeping socialism and all its evils. But we have too seldom devoted ourselves to an open-minded examination of the problems, aspirations, and difficulties of millions of our citizens seeking to make meaningful lives in a complex society.

We have been interested (to the voters we *seem* to have been interested) more in capitalizing on the faults of the Democrats than in helping insure a strong and stable economy whose products would be used for the greatest spiritual and material good of the greatest number. Too many Republican leaders have attacked not only the blunders of the New Deal, the Fair Deal, the New Frontier, and the Great Society (and there have been many blunders to attack), but also their enlightened innovations, innovations that the overwhelming majority of Americans consider essential. Like the generals of World War I, these leaders have become wedded to the tactics of defense in an age of political offense. Where are *our* plans for a New Deal or a Great Society? Where are our alternatives?

That those Republicans dedicated to blanket opposition were wrong has been demonstrated not only by our poor performance at the polls since 1930, but even stronger proof has been produced by our own reaction to Democratic innovations during the few years we were in power. We did not dismantle Democratic programs — that would have led to disaster. On the contrary, we continued to operate them as they were designed. We made important improvements in a wide variety of programs. We extended social security, wrote pioneering civil rights legislation and in general made the administration of many programs more rational and efficient. But on the whole, we accepted the Democratic framework. And even our improvements, in a perverse way, sometimes weakened our image. For we were reduced to improving Democratic programs, programs that many of us bitterly attacked when first proposed. Worse: we were forced to campaign in an awkward manner. "Oh, no," we assured the voters, "we're not against social security or unemployment compensation or the T.V.A. You see, we were never *really* against these things, it's just that . . ."

So strong is our image as critics and "standpatters" that we have received almost no credit for those significant innovations and improvements we did make. How many remember the Republicans' 1957 legislation that established the United States Civil Rights Commission? And how many remember the expansion of the social security program under President Eisenhower to include many categories of Americans hitherto deprived of its benefits? Or that several outstanding Republicans in Congress fought to extend the Medicare program to senior citizens not protected by social security? These achievements are lost in the deluge of Democratic proposals. It is simply and erroneously assumed by millions of voters that Republicans oppose social progress, that we could not have made the contributions that in fact we have made.

The greatest weakness of contemporary Republicanism is that it is known not for what it proposes — it proposes too little — but for its dogged determination to speak out *against* the proposals of others. We are known as people who substitute negativism — a grumbling, carping, protesting rejection of new ideas — for constructive policies. It is felt that we practice the politics of futility. We are pictured as being dragged, kicking and screaming, into new times with new social and economic arrangements established by Democrats. A defensive party produces no great ideas and no great leaders. We have had too few of both in these last decades. Among those Republicans who will be mentioned in future history textbooks, many will be remembered for their willingness, after long reluctance, to cooperate with Democrats as junior partners, helping to make Democratic ideas work.

Samuel Lubell has described our plight succinctly. "Since the depression, Republican political strategy has been dominated by *one* driving motive — a hunt for issues or candidates which would divert popular attention from this weakness on bread and work issues. . . . Until the GOP regains its economic nerve it is doubtful that it can serve as a truly stable and constructive party." Our weakness on "bread and work" issues, as Mr. Lubell calls them, forces us to grasp at straws in a desperate effort to capitalize on peripheral issues.

I think this argument has been overstated. I believe that Republicans are not barren of ideas. To the voters, however, we *seem* to be barren of ideas. No matter what we think we are saying, the majority of voters hear us saying "no." "No, but . . ." "No, because . . ." but principally "no." And by saying "no" we seem to be dismissing not only Democratic proposals but the real and disturbing conditions that inspired them. We seem irritated, timid,

[49]

fearful — out of step with the times. No matter how we feel, we give the appearance of being afraid of social progress. This is what has made us known as the cold party, the party of the upper classes, the party without humanity. And this, more than anything, has reduced us to our perennial minority status. We are offering too little to too many beyond weary, sterile slogans.

And this is what we must set about to change.

SIX

America during the Republican Decline

OUR problems are grave, our prospects somber. It is
difficult for many of us to admit to our disorders —
but more difficult still to agree to the cures. What can we
do to restore the party's vigor? Will we be able to make
creative responses to the challenge of defeat? Obviously
we must make a response of some sort; simple logic dictates we cannot stand pat or rest on our laurels. A minority party must take the verdict of the voters into account
or forever remain a minority or become extinct, suffering
the fate of the Federalists and Whigs, both former opponents of the Democrats.

If we fail to make creative changes, we will win an election now and then when the Democrats bungle affairs
disastrously, and there might even come a time (such as
the decade following World War I) when the country,
tired of social progress, seeks a period of consolidation.
These will be our opportunities. But they will be negative
and temporary opportunities that provide little hope of
offering anything creative or distinguished. And the time
will follow shortly when the country is again eager to
move forward. For no social and economic order is perfect,

and no people is permanently satisfied with the status quo. Unless we accommodate ourselves to this forward motion and prepare ourselves to lead it, rather than to tread water in its wake, we face more decades of consistent defeats.

The crucial question is, where do we go from here? Assuming we agree on the need for changes, what ought to be their nature? I think we should first examine the nature of the country's changes. What has been happening to America during the years of the Republican decline? Where is *it* going from here?

To answer the question "what has been happening to America?" is to attempt to describe one of the most remarkable social and economic transformations in history. From a pastoral land of small farms and small shops, we have become an intensely industrialized colossus of giant cities and corporations. From a country which offered isolation and the opportunity to escape and prosper on its frontier, we have become the land of instant communication and continuous interaction. From a people raised in large families separated by wide distances and economic independence, we have been transformed into a nation of families pushed in tight one upon the other at work and at home, almost totally dependent upon one another (and upon peoples elsewhere in the world) for our comforts, our peace of mind, even our daily bread. The American "paradise of small farms, each man secure on his own freehold," as the historian Arthur Schlesinger, Jr., has described it, has ceased to exist (if ever it existed at all) except in our imaginations. We have become a clamorous, prosperous urban nation, where national television commercials have superseded the door-to-door peddler, stupendous assembly lines have superseded the village blacksmith, billion-dollar supermarket chains have superseded the corner grocer, and the need for the individual to find a niche in this world of giants has superseded the urge to "go it alone." Very little of what we once did for ourselves can now be done without intimate contact with the economic and social giants of our society. America has literally been remade in this century.

The effects of this transformation are so profound and comprehensive that I cannot hope to outline them here, even superficially. Our homes, our habits, our families, our work, our play, our way of thinking, our very way of life have been substantially transformed. Only a few of us plow our own fields and gather our daily living with our own hands from the soil. We work for someone else (often "someone" we never actually see), together with hundreds or thousands of others, in factories and offices. We travel home on crowded subways and highways, worrying about raises, pensions and unemployment. Business and government record us as digits on their computers. Our lives are compartmentalized both as producers and consumers: we deal less and less as "whole men" with the forces of nature, and more and more as specialists in narrow fields with man-made corporations, conditions and procedures.

This is a fundamental change in our pattern of living which has followed the natural laws of economic development. Nothing can undo it. We can pine for the past; we can convince ourselves that the old way of life was more virtuous and romantic. But we cannot return to it any more than we can return to an undiscovered America. We can-

not unlearn the techniques of mass production, dismantle
our industrial complexes and our cities, or stop super-
markets from spreading. For better or worse, forces beyond our control have made us a nation primarily of
factory and office workers, apartment dwellers and suburbanites. The best we can do is to recognize that this, and
not the old homestead, has become the American way of
life.

Of course the transformation from farm to factory,
country to city, self-sufficiency to interdependence began
well before the Republican decline, even before the twentieth century. But the changes have accelerated markedly
in the past several decades. It was the 1920 census which
disclosed that more Americans were living in cities than
in the country for the first time. Thereafter, the migration
rapidly gained momentum. Now, some two-thirds of our
population live in metropolitan areas, and by 1970, just
after the next presidential election, it is estimated that the
figure will be eighty per cent. Statistics tend to be tedious, so I will repeat this one in other terms: by the beginning of the next decade, four out of five of the predicted
two hundred and fifty million Americans will be living in urban centers, with all that implies in terms of their
daily lives, their problems and their political persuasions.
"It is commonplace," wrote V. O. Key, "that American
cities have grown rapidly, yet it is difficult to grasp the
magnitude of the change in our way of life and the almost cataclysmic political consequences of urbanization."
The old order changeth; and in America, changeth fast.

But political changes lag behind economic and social
changes. Although the effects of industrialization and ur-

banization were obvious before the 1930's, it was only then that America's political response to them materialized. The New Deal marked the beginning of the change. One can argue that the New Deal was born prematurely because of the shock of the Depression, or that its coming was postponed because of World War I and the euphoric optimism of the 1920's. Whatever the merits of these arguments, something like the New Deal was certain to arrive sooner or later. Some increased measure of government participation in the workings of the economy — to stimulate economic growth, to encourage stability, to help channel the nation's wealth toward cultural, ethical, political and social goals, and to protect the individual against the hazards of impersonal economic forces — was inevitable. These measures are indispensable to every free-enterprise society. Every Western nation has the equivalent of its New Deal; every successful economic system in the mid-twentieth century is in some measure "mixed." Every government of every nation we call free takes upon itself a greater or lesser responsibility for regulating, collaborating with, and inspiring private enterprise to work within a framework of national values.

There was nothing extraordinary or unnatural about the coming of the New Deal. On the contrary, it, too, followed the natural laws of America's economic development. Fundamental economic and social transformations have always required corresponding political changes. The urbanization and industrialization of America gave us enormous wealth and blessings. But, inevitably, they also gave us a whole spectrum of new and quantitatively different problems. Great poverty and hopelessness were produced along with great wealth. Catastrophic depressions alternated with speculative booms. Lives were stunted and ruined while others prospered. Parts of the country were given over to ugliness while other parts flowered. The notion that, left to itself, the law of supply and demand of the marketplace would automatically regulate the economy and develop the nation in accordance with the finest values of civilization, was shattered by a quite different reality. And above all, the hope that the individual — all individuals — could make meaningful lives for themselves and their families in this new world of concrete and machinery without encouragement and protection by government was found to be illusory. Inevitably, government assumed additional responsibilities in order to discharge its constitutional obligation to "promote the general welfare."

No one wanted big government for its own sake. No one wanted big business, big labor, or big farming either. But just as big economic units provided advantages of protection, efficiency and profit, big government provided advantages of protection, prevention of abuse, and progress toward human betterment. There are advantages to both bigness and smallness, and in the best of all possible worlds perhaps we would choose the latter, in our government as well as in our economic institutions. But we no longer have that choice. The bigness of industrialization came upon us with all of its blessings and problems, and big government inevitably followed.

No man lives by himself, the contemporary American least of all. Even the few of us who still work our own farms cannot provide for opportunity, progress and beauty without encouragement by government. No individual can, for example, cope with the effects of water and air pollution. And in the cities we are even less independent. Few Americans can individually test the purity of food and drugs, insure ourselves against depression and unemployment, protect ourselves against abuses by big business and big labor, or provide the resources for our recreation and comfort, even for the neighborhood playground and parks. Industrialization and urbanization introduced literally hundreds of problems with which no individual, and even few cities and states, can cope alone. They are, many of them, truly national problems and can be dealt with effectively only by the whole nation.

In a world of giant economic establishments operating in accordance with impersonal economic laws, the individual felt lost. Quite naturally, he turned to government for encouragement and protection. But government provided more than just protection against abuse. Government was no longer limited merely to the solution of old problems. New problems developed and, more important, Americans began to expect their government to solve them. The concept of positive, creative government emerged and made its way into American traditions.

And herein lies the most significant change since the Republican decline from power. The expectations of Americans, their concept of what constitutes a meaningful and comfortable life, have risen steadily throughout these decades, both in terms of the goods and services provided by business and in terms of the services and protections provided by government. Owning a car was once a dream; now a second car seems a necessity. Television sets, domestic luxuries and conveniences, variety of clothes, and lengths and distances of vacations fit the same pattern. And so do expectations of government. A high school diploma was once a cherished ambition; now a higher degree is very nearly a necessity. And garbage collection, public health, adequate social security pensions — everything from modern sewage to modern air-traffic systems — fit the same pattern.

Is it unnatural to expect more and better services by government? We expect more and better of everything else. Is it unnatural for government budgets to grow? Our personal budgets and the budgets of America's great corporations are growing. The "good things in life" are not limited to the ownership of material *things*. They include parks, programs for cultural development, and protection against unemployment — the kinds of services government is best able to provide. As we get richer, we want more of everything that contributes to well-rounded lives, not only to our material possessions.

What happened in the 1930's was nothing less than the emergence of a new attitude toward government. Americans saw what the New Deal could do — at least what it was attempting to do — and the majority of them approved. There are a great many things that government can *not* do and should not do, such as providing the traditional goods and services of the marketplace. For this — for the design, manufacture, distribution and sale of industrial and consumer products — American business has created a superb system, unequaled and even unapproached anywhere else in the world. But for the services which business, by nature, is unequipped to provide, Americans quite naturally began to expect help from their government.

Throughout American history, there had always been slums, poverty, disease, lack of education and lack of recreation. There had always been unemployment, mental sickness, racial discrimination, overcrowding and ugliness — in short, something less than an opportunity for each individual citizen to develop to his full potential. But Americans began to feel that government had a vital role in solving these problems. Standards were raised and horizons widened; not just sweatshops, rats in slums and twelve-hour days for factory children concerned the nation, but improvement of the quality of life at every level.

The forces of social reform are irresistible. It is in the nature of things American and human to move forward; it is an integral element of progress. Call it democratization, humanization, or civilization, whatever one chooses, it is a continuation of the traditional American expansion of opportunity which soon, we hope, will make the Good Life available to all.

The expansion of opportunity has progressed, with stops and starts, since the founding of the Republic. One tends to forget that when the Republic was established, many states had a constitutional requirement for ownership of property as proof that a citizen merited the privilege of voting. As the interpretation of civic justice widened, that restriction was found to be intolerable. A century or so later, we still held to the notion that no legislature could establish rules for the hours and conditions of factory work. That restriction crumbled, too, as the concept of democracy widened. Now, in this spirit, we are finding poverty, slums, wasted lives, ugliness, and lost opportunity to be intolerable in the midst of plenty. As our resources, standards, expectations, and interpretation of democracy expand, we make expanded demands upon government. It is unreal to imagine that our demands upon government will shrink. We want to improve the quality of our lives, not leave well enough alone (nothing is ever "well enough," especially for Americans), and certainly not retreat.

I believe that much of what government has done in the last thirty-five years *has* improved our lives. But what I think is secondary to this argument. The essential fact — verified by all too many elections — is that most Americans believe the measures which began with the New Deal improved their lives.

These are fundamental changes that have overtaken America in the years of the Republican decline. There has been a population increase of almost sixty per cent. There has been a vast increase in personal and corporate wealth. There has been an intensification of industrialization and urbanization, and beyond this, there has been a recognition by most Americans that in this bountiful yet fretful new society government must play the role of a partner to private enterprise. It must do what must be done, but what our private enterprise cannot do. And at the same time, it must encourage us to accomplish what we can do privately, but have not. This is not entirely a new role. The granting of a hundred and forty thousand college scholarships to needy students is, after all, merely an extension of the principle of free universal high school education to deal with new needs and circumstances. But even though some aspects of the role *are* new, this is no cause for fear. When American states first established free grammar schools, that idea was new too; we were the first nation in the world to test it. It was a change for the better, and it was quickly recognized as such. So too were most of the changes of recent decades.

And where is America going from here? Further, I believe, in the same direction of economic and social change. Demographers predict that urbanization will level off at some point after eighty per cent of our population have settled in metropolitan centers. And industrialization will level off too, at least in the strict sense of the word. Actually, in terms of percentage of workers employed in factories, industrialization has already declined from its peak. As mechanization and automation proceed, fewer workers will be needed to man more complex machines.

But these trends will only increase demands upon government. They will intensify pressures to improve the standards of education, recreation, and city living. In the broadest sense, industrialization and urbanization are in their infancy. Social scientists warn that the coming decades will bring more profound changes in the American way of life — in our habits of work and living — than any we have yet experienced. We are not returning to our pastoral past; on the contrary, the underlying social and economic trends of the past thirty years are accelerating in a geometric progression. We are becoming more automatized and more urbanized — more populous, affluent and interdependent. This requires more positive action by government; more concern for the solution of new, complex problems, more creativity to satisfy growing needs and adjust to social forces. Bigger government is not necessarily the answer, but better government surely is.

Perhaps American society will somehow rearrange itself during some future century so that we can return not to small farms and shops but to new forms of individual, independent endeavor. That kind of society, however, can now be envisaged only in science fiction. For the present, the American way of life will continue to be lived in vast social and economic concentrations — the metropolis and the corporation. And the duty of government will continue to be the improvement of that life.

SEVEN

✤ ✤ ✤

Betrayal of Republican Tradition

THE relationship between the changes in American society and the decline of the Republican Party is, I am
afraid, all too apparent. The painful truth is that most
voters feel the Republican Party has been second-best in
dealing with the issues of this era. They say the Democratic Party, either by instinct, intelligence or simple
political expediency, has done more to understand and liberate, to work with and capitalize upon the great underlying economic and social forces which have been remaking
mid-twentieth-century America.

Democrats did not create these forces any more than
Republicans created the forces that remade America in
the Age of Enterprise following the Civil War. Nor did
government itself create them. They were no more or no
less than a product of the times, flowing from all that was
happening in that era: discoveries, inventions, resources,
immigration, developments in law, technology and economics, influence of social tracts, labor movements, business techniques, and above all, the currents of intellectual
thought in a nation undergoing a particular kind of change
dictated by a particular era. No party and no free gov-

ernment could create these forces. They were the work of Henry Ford, Jack London, John D. Rockefeller, Walter Reuther, and millions of lesser known men who discovered uses for petroleum in laboratories, crusaded for the ten-hour day at union rallies, or simply toiled and yearned. These forces are history's products, not the brainstorm of any one man, party or government.

But the first task of government and of parties aspiring to govern is to understand them. To accommodate them with the past and its older social and economic forces, to channel them into meaningful directions, to fit them into established political processes, to encourage the good in them and discourage the bad, to make the transition as painless as possible, and to seek arrangements for them that will bring the greatest good to the greatest number. The essence of statesmanship is not to oppose these great forces — for they cannot be successfully opposed — but to bend them toward ends which benefit the public welfare. A successful party rolls up its sleeves and works with the forces of its times, rather than bemoaning their potential harm.

Before Republicans can begin to mold America as *we* would like it to be, we must first recognize America as it is. We must concern ourselves with where and how Americans now live, rather than where and how they used to live. The paradox is that Republicans were more responsible than anyone else for establishing how and where Americans now live. The early Republicans played the leading role in creating our mass industrialized society and the enlightened capitalism that followed it. Many Republican leaders, however, failed to adjust to the society that early Republican statesmen were so instrumental in molding.

A great deal has been written and said recently about ailing Republicanism, most of it designed to demonstrate that the party is inherently unequipped to deal with change. "Immobile," "paralyzed," "embedded in rigid conservatism" — these qualities are being ascribed to us as if intrinsic to our very nature. My own opinion is that we have not contended adequately with the most significant social and economic changes since the 1930's. But it is a great mistake — a mistake unfortunately often made by Republicans themselves — to assume that resistance to change is ordained by the spirit of the Republican Party.

What is the spirit of the Republican Party? At its birth the spirit was progressive and reformist; the renowned historians Samuel Eliot Morison and Henry Steele Commager have described the initial Republican atmosphere as a "flush of radicalism." The party was founded, as the Civil War approached, to meet an urgent need for *change.* It sprung up spontaneously, the "most powerful, authentic grass roots movement in American political history" to deal — justly, at last — with the issue of slavery. "*Resolved,*" agreed the few thousand citizens who formed the first Republican "convention" in Jackson, Michigan, in 1854, "that in view of the necessity of battling for the first principles of Republican government, and against the schemes of an aristocracy, the most revolting and oppressive with which the earth was ever cursed, or man debased, we will cooperate and be known as *Republicans* until the contest be terminated." This served as the state-

[65]

ment of principle for the creation of the Republican Party.

Today there are daily references to the party's "traditional" role as standpatters and protectors of the status quo. But the historical fact is that the first Republicans were reformers. "Convinced that the cause of freedom must support a new party," in Morison and Commager's words, they banded together to battle the narrow, selfish, antidemocratic conservatism of the Democratic Party. "The spirit of the first Republicans," writes Professor Rossiter, "was essentially progressive, democratic, even radical; the party itself was based as much on ideals as on interests. Whatever the Republicans were to become in later years, they were far from being a conservative, business-oriented party in infancy." To be sure, the party's spirit has been changed between 1854 and 1964. But to say that resistance to social change is rooted in the origins of Republicanism is simply bad history. We sometimes hear talk of a betrayal of Republican tradition. It should be understood that rigid opposition to change, not willingness to innovate, is the betrayal.

I wish there were an effective way of publicizing the origin of the Republican Party to the nation. So much misleading commentary is now made or implied that most Americans are understandably confused. The facts are quite different from the popular conception of them. Republicanism was born an amalgam of many seemingly disparate elements, but its prevailing orientation, if one can speak of a prevailing orientation in any American party, was primarily to the interests of the working man and the intellectuals. As Republicans won control of state legislatures in the 1860's, they devoted themselves to writing pi-

oneering, although at that time rudimentary, labor legislation. In Congress, Republicans established the prece-
dent for federal aid to education by creating state agricultural colleges (in the Morrill Act of 1862); and for federal
encouragement of higher scholarship by founding the National Academy of Sciences in 1863. The Republican Party
quickly became the national progressive party, committed
to using the powers of government creatively and imaginatively to encourage the expansion of the country, its
powerful industrial forces, and its democratic ideas.

As for democratic ideas, no American politician is more
intimately associated with them than President Lincoln.
Lincoln's political philosophy was complex and defies simple categorization. Yet I think it fair to assume that were
he placed in our present political context, he would lead a
determined Republican attack on the problems of racial
inequality, urban deterioration, and poverty here and
abroad.

Lincoln spoke clearly about the responsibility of American government, the primary obligation of the Republican Party and the duty of both to accommodate to social
and economic change. "The legitimate object of government," he said, "is to do for a community of people whatever they need to have done, but cannot do at all, or
cannot do so well for themselves, in their separate and individual capacities." "Republicans are for both the man and
the dollar," he said later, "but in case of conflict, the man
before the dollar." And, near his death: "The dogmas of
the quiet past are inadequate to the stormy present. As
our cause is new, so must we think anew, and act anew.
We must disenthrall ourselves and then we shall save the
country."

[67]

With these as his central premises about the obligation of the party to use the powers of government as an instrument of social betterment, Lincoln helped engineer a series of bold innovations. Not all, not even most of his innovations were reformist in the sense of protection for laborers and poor farmers. There was attention to that, but there was also the Banking Act of 1864, which gave the United States a stable, universal currency, the promotion of the transcontinental railroad, tariff reforms to protect new industries and higher paid American labor, the Homestead Act, which encouraged settlement of the West, and, as mentioned, the establishment of the National Academy of Sciences and the land-grant agricultural colleges.

Lincoln's purpose in directing these reforms, which at the time were "daring and radical," was to mold social and economic changes toward the national interest. The problems he faced were complex, and his responses to them were subtle and varied. But I think one can speak of a common approach to Lincoln's response: a willingness to innovate. Lincoln was a conservative in the sense that he worked, above all, to preserve the Union and its political establishment. He was careful to accommodate change to tradition. But when tradition and traditional methods were irrelevant to new issues, he did not hesitate to use new methods and ideas. He was masterful in translating social pressures into constructive national programs.

The Republican Party dominated American politics in the thirty-five years following the Civil War more completely than the Democratic Party has dominated during the last thirty-five years. It cannot be fairly said that after President Lincoln's assassination most leading Republican politicians were distinguished by dedication to social progress. As the nation and especially the nation's great industrial corporations expanded, there was often ruthlessness in the pursuit of self-interest, and callous disregard for the hardships of the many amidst the enrichment of the few. But there was also an incredibly dynamic economic growth and development of human energy and ingenuity, and an unparalleled transformation of America from an agricultural country to the world's greatest industrial power. And it was the Republican Party, far more than the Democratic, that liberated and guided these immense forces.

This was an age of invention, enterprise and industrial empire-building, and if there was too little attention to abuses such as child labor and starvation wages, that was as much the fault of the times as of the Republican Party. Democrats were no more successful in coping with the hardships of industrialization than Republicans. The great social and economic forces of the post–Civil War era centered about the development of America's natural, rather than human, resources; and consciously or instinctively, for self-interest or national interest, Republicans helped fertilize and nurture these forces. Business was the predominant spirit of this era. Republicans were predominant because they embodied this spirit. No one can say that the age of enterprise provided prosperity for the working man's family, but it did provide the economic machinery for universal prosperity in succeeding generations.

The death of President McKinley marked the end of this

[69]

explosive, rapacious era. "Not only was he the last President who had served in the Civil War," wrote George Mayer, a Republican historian, "but the last one to believe that America's problems were simply and easily solved. Like most of his generation, he had no real comprehension of the squalor and misery that lurked beneath the surface of national prosperity."

A new era was born with the new century, and its spirit was captured by the new Republican President better than any other statesman in the country. Theodore Roosevelt was both a symbol and a shaper of twentieth-century America. Appalled by the Republicans who had been controlling Congress (he called them "reactionaries . . . who for various reasons . . . distrusted anything that was progressive"), he made the Republican Party an agency of social progress, and helped reshape the nation in accordance with the forces of reform which were sweeping the world. The Theodore Roosevelt era was one of the most forceful, productive and rewarding periods in the party's development.

So much of the basic foundation of government's functions in the twentieth century was laid by Theodore Roosevelt's administration that it is difficult even to outline the accomplishments. And so accepted have his innovations now become that it is difficult to demonstrate their novelty and the bitter resistance they inspired as "radical schemes." President Roosevelt responded to the problems of old age, sickness, starvation wages and inhuman working hours, unemployment, squalid slums and other by-products of the new industrial age as no other politician of his time. His purpose was to give Americans the means to help themselves in an industrial age. But if this sounds like a cliché, his concrete legislative and administrative reforms were anything but clichés. They were masterful works that translated the social and economic forces of the new age into new institutions and procedures vital to the great masses of primarily immigrant voters.

"Welfare" used in connection with "government" now has a Democratic ring, but many tend to forget that Theodore Roosevelt was the first American statesman to announce that government must become an "agent of human welfare." The "deals" of American politics — the New Deal, Fair Deal, New Frontier, the Great Society — sound "Democratic" too. But many also forget that the first of the "deals" was a Republican institution. It was Theodore Roosevelt's Square Deal, an approach to the role of government as sound and inspiring as any of the subsequent Democratic programs which borrowed from it.

"When I say I am for the square deal," said Roosevelt in 1910, "I mean not merely that I stand for fair play under the present rules of the game, but I stand for having those rules changed so as to work for a more substantial equality of opportunity. . . . The true conservative is the one who insists that property shall be the servant and not the master of the commonwealth. . . . The citizens of the United States must effectively control the mighty commercial forces which they have themselves called into being. . . . This, I know implies a policy of far more active government interference with social and economic conditions in this country than we have yet had, but I think we have got to face the fact that such an increase in governmental control is now necessary. . . . The betterment which we seek must be accomplished, I believe, mainly through the National Government. The American people are right in demanding the New Nationalism without which we cannot cope with the new problems. . . . I believe in shaping the ends of government to protect property as well as human life. Normally, and in the long run, the ends are the same; but whenever the alternative must be faced, I am for men and not for property."

Here was a positive, self-confident statement about government's role as an instrument of social progress and its duty to help "the individual cast adrift in the great society." It was not a new theory of the state so much as a restatement of the traditional function of government in terms relevant to the new economic and social forces of an industrializing country.

Theodore Roosevelt's administration set precedents that have become indispensable to America's development. There was federal support for irrigation and land reclamation, extension of national forest preserves, and inauguration of a splendid tradition of conservation. There was increased regulation of imperious financial and industrial trusts, railroads, and banks; support for hard-pressed working men and their struggle to unionize; creation of the Department of Commerce; and a strengthening of regulation of interstate commerce. There was sponsorship of the Pure Food and Drug Act, encouragement to state legislatures struggling to enact humane labor laws, reform of the civil, consular and Indian services, vast improvement of the merchant marine, and more generous support to the Smithsonian Institution.

There were literally dozens of programs designed, as President Roosevelt put it, to establish "methods of controlling the big corporations without paralyzing the energies of the business community." Above all, there was a willingness to channel the restless forces of reform and justice for the working man into concrete solutions to concrete problems. "Neither this people or any other free people," Roosevelt said in 1905, "will permanently tolerate the use of the vast power conferred by vast wealth without lodging somewhere in government the still higher power of seeing that this power is used for and not against the interests of the people as a whole."

Roosevelt was not anti-business. "Our aim," he explained, "is not to do away with corporations; on the contrary, these big aggregations are an inevitable development of modern industrialism. . . . We are not attacking the corporations, but endeavoring to do away with any evil in them." He was not *against* business, but for its development in ways which would enhance the general well-being of the nation. He rode herd on the great forces of his time: the legitimate aspirations of masses of Americans to share the benefits and opportunities of the industrial age. He used the office of the presidency to the full extent of its then more limited powers — and extended those powers to deal with new dilemmas. Nor was he apologetic about extending presidential or governmental powers in general. "The man who wrongly holds that every human right is secondary to his profit must give way to the advocate of human welfare, who rightly maintains that every man holds his property subject to the general right of the community to regulate its use to whatever degree the public welfare may require it."

Our contemporary problems are not the same as they were during Theodore Roosevelt's administration, but his approach to government is more relevant now than at the turn of the century.

My objective is not a history of the Republican Party but an analysis of its present difficulties. Those to whom Republicanism and good government mean something different from what they mean to me can muster as many pertinent quotes to support their arguments as I can to support mine. They might quote President Calvin Coolidge, for example: "If the Federal Government should go out of existence," he said, "the common run of people would not detect the difference in the affairs of their daily life for a considerable length of time. . . . The law that builds up people is the law that builds up industry. . . . The business of the United States is business." Or they might quote President Warren G. Harding: "The sole function of government is to bring about a condition of affairs favorable to the beneficial development of private enterprise." Or they might quote scores of outstanding contemporary Republican leaders who feel, as one of them graphically put it, that governmental activity is "poison ivy in the garden of industry." But citations of this sort solve little, for there is always a surplus of them on all sides of all issues to support one's arguments and predilections.

Those of us who have differing notions about the direction the party should take are like lawyers presenting a line of cases in a legal argument. The learned counsel on the "other side" does not lack precedents or logic. The decision as to which precedents are more persuasive — which approach to government will be more beneficial for the country and rewarding for the party — will be left to the judges, present Republicans and millions of non-Republicans who I hope may be encouraged to join the Republican Party. My purpose here is merely to point out at this critical time in the party's history that there has always existed in Republicanism a strong strain of liberalism, modernism, progressivism, intellectualism — of capacity and eagerness to lead the nation by working with the forces of social change. This strain runs deep in the Republican Party. Present appearances to the contrary notwithstanding, it lies at the very core of the Republican tradition.

And I think it can be demonstrated that the most successful Republican statesmen — successful both in terms of popular approval and the appraisal of historians — were those who drew their inspiration principally from this strain. Presidents Lincoln and Roosevelt, Chief Justice Charles Evans Hughes, Secretaries Elihu Root, Henry Stimson and Republicans like them, I believe, have done most for the nation and, coincidentally, for the party. Perhaps President Eisenhower cannot be said to have drawn his inspiration directly from this strain of Republicanism, but he and his staff were deeply influenced by it. And I suppose there is no need to remind ourselves of the providential luck which sent us President Eisenhower. For even though his accomplishments were not great in rebuilding the party at grass roots, local and state levels, it is probable that without him, the Republican Party would have been reduced to controlling just a single session of Congress and not a single presidential administration in the last thirty-four years.

I have made these brief references to the "progressive" strain in Republican history more to remind readers that it exists than to convince them that it is correct. For in this period of floundering, its existence is obscure to millions of American voters, especially young voters, including young Republican voters. Theodore White, one of America's most perceptive political writers, has observed that "now that the Democrats have captured the liberal imagination of the nation, it has forgotten how much of the architecture of America's liberal society was drafted by the Republicans. . . . This is the party that abolished slavery, wrote the first laws of civil service, passed the first antitrust, railway control, consumer-protective and conservation legislation, and then led America, with enormous diplomatic skill, out into that posture of global leadership and responsibility we now so desperately try to maintain . . . down through [the] first decade [of the twentieth century] the natural home of the American intellectual, writer, savant and artist was the Republican Party."

Many young voters I meet are skeptical when I talk about these aspects of Republicanism. Many young Republicans, poorly informed about the party's history, assume that our present stance is our natural, historical one. Many zealous, right-wing young Republicans assume they are defending Republican tradition by attacking bold, creative use of governmental powers to further social ends. In fact, they are not upholding Republican tradition, but undermining it.

But I mention Republican history principally to appeal to those tens of millions of Democrats and Independents who are convinced that it is "only natural," somehow, that the Republican Party is negative and stubborn — always afraid to act for fear of upsetting the status quo, always "against everything." This is simply not true. It has not always been this way, and it need not be this way. An eagerness to meet the challenge of change, to innovate, to channel new social and economic forces with new political institutions — these are not at all alien to the spirit of the Republican Party. On the contrary, they are entirely in harmony with the spirit of the party, at least with the spirit that made the party great.

✦ ✦ ✦

The Era of Republican Negativism

WITH diligent search and the benefit of retrospection, one can find historical causes for the present Republican difficulty as far back as the formation of the party a century ago. For together with the dynamic spirit personified by Presidents Lincoln and Roosevelt, there were other tendencies in the party which worked to lower its capacity to lead the nation in periods of change. But this has always been true of all American parties. The direct sources of the present Republican predicament are to be found, I believe, in the decade of "normalcy" following World War I.

It was a decade of prosperity, good times and frivolity when national problems gave promise of solving themselves if only government would leave them alone. To a dangerous extent, the prosperity was based on a shoddy financial foundation and on speculation. Morison and Commager called it "a florid but badly distributed industrial prosperity accompanied by agricultural distress and succeeded by acute and prolonged depression." But that was apparent only with hindsight. At the time, people were exhilarated by the development of the automobile and radio, the expansion of industry and services, the satisfying of consumer demand pent-up during the war and stimulated further by the exuberance of the era. Things seemed wonderful and getting even more so, and in the absence of serious crises, the Republican philosophy seemed to prove its merit. Let everything alone! Let the people do it themselves! Let business alone!

"This is a business country," said President Coolidge, ". . . and it wants a business government." The business governments of Presidents Harding, Coolidge and Hoover were built around a cardinal tenet: Government must not interfere. A myth developed that government was to be feared as something alien, not respected as something positive. Government was considered mischievious at best, and at worst — which was all too often — it was a sinister enemy of the people, forever seeking to destroy, in President Herbert Hoover's words, "something infinitely valuable" in the American character. There was little creative thinking and little planning, beyond a determination to let free enterprise set the tone of national life. Those Republicans who proposed government action to solve the problems of the period (for in spite of prosperity, there were serious problems) were called "tinkerers," "statistists," or "radicals." Government inaction was elevated from a principle to an article of faith, and finally to a dogma: the "natural laws of economics," it was claimed, would regulate everything to make the best of all possible worlds, and no mortals should attempt to interfere. If government were to act, except to lower taxes and raise tariffs, it would only spoil our system and virtues. Worse: it would violate God-given, immutable laws of economics and bring about Divine retribution.

It was a plausible doctrine in that implausible decade, and the Democrats, divided as usual, were offering nothing better. The doctrine seemed to work — not magnificently well, but at least as well, in that postwar industrialization boom, as anything known before. Happily, Republican majorities seemed to produce themselves. In a perverse sense, it was unfortunate that Republicans were so successful during the 1920's, which was a calm before the storm. In that brief era, the party's progressive spirit sharply declined. The unfortunate consequences of the decline were not immediately apparent, for the progressive spirit in the country as a whole declined. But the consequences — the complacency, the rigidity, the blind faith in business — were soon to cause the party's undoing.

For those who cared to examine the voting trends, it was already apparent that the traditional sources of Republican majorities — "the coalition of Midwestern farmers, big business and the old middle class" — were in the process of being overwhelmed by a new coalition of Southern and Northern minority groups, based largely on the urban working class. The erosion of Republican support in the fastest-growing areas was demonstrated clearly in 1928: the country's dozen largest cities, which had produced a Republican plurality of nearly a million and a half votes in 1924, swung to the Democrats. The new Democratic voters in the cities looked to government as an instrument for bettering their lives. But Republican leaders, self-confident after their three successive presidential victories, largely ignored the underlying change in American voting habits. Victorious, they saw no need to change the old winning formula. When catastrophe, in the form of the Great Depression, struck, the dogma of government noninterference became a dead weight tied to a sinking party. "In their hour of adversity," as Robert Donovan has put it, "all their sins of omission of the 1920's were there to plague them."

At first, the leaders of the party reacted to the Depression by assuring everyone there was nothing really wrong. "Leave things alone," they said, "and they will right themselves." The Depression was an optical illusion — or, if not that, an infection from abroad. Meanwhile, a third of the American labor force was unemployed, and many Americans were literally starving. President Hoover did try to act, but his pragmatic engineer's mind was hobbled by the doctrine of the evil of government intervention. The theory of automatic adjustment by a self-regulating business mechanism held sway. Antipathy to positive government action, and particularly to anything that smacked of innovation, was too deeply rooted to be shed even in the face of 1929's appalling disaster. (The disaster was unlike anything America had ever experienced: from 1929 to 1932, manufacturing income fell from seven billion to two billion dollars, and corporate profits fell from eleven billion to two billion dollars.) President Hoover pledged ever and ever greater reduction in government spending, when the opposite was desperately needed; and the party headquarters proclaimed that "Republicans are firm in their belief that a violation of well-established, sound economic principles . . . will . . . result in even greater disaster."

The times cried out for something new, something experimental, something humane. But President Hoover defended the old orthodoxies — the gold standard, the protective tariff, the balanced budget — as the three corner-

[81]

stones of Republican policy. The accumulated rigidity of the decade before the crash had convinced leading Republicans that no matter how bad the country's situation, the danger of government action was even greater. President Hoover vetoed a bill proposing government operation of the power plant at Muscle Shoals, site of the future T.V.A.; he vetoed the Wagner Bill to extend federal employment agencies to states that had no agencies of their own; and he refused to provide direct relief to bankrupt farmers ruined by the crash and the dust bowl. These measures were proposed by a small group of Republicans working with a minority of Democrats (most Democrats were then as rigidly orthodox as most Republicans), but they were opposed by the administration on the grounds that action by the federal government would interfere with state control over problems like unemployment, and that the federal government was not responsible for providing "gifts" to relieve human suffering.

Let it be remembered that the Democrats of those days had nothing better to offer. They too — at least the majority of Democratic congressmen — were bewildered and negative. After all, this was a new kind of calamity for which almost all politicians were unprepared. Candidate Franklin D. Roosevelt, too, during his presidential campaigning in 1932, promised a reduction in government spending.

And let it also be remembered that the Democrats were lucky: they were in the blessed role of opposition when the worst economic disaster of our history struck the country. Of course, no one can prove that the Depression would have occurred had the Democrats been in power, but most historians feel it is reasonable to expect it would have. And had it occurred with Democrats in power, no doubt they too would have felt compelled to defend their earlier administrations, to insist that things were not as bad as they seemed, and to fall back on old orthodoxies which had now so obviously failed.

But that, of course, was not what happened. When candidate Roosevelt became President Roosevelt, he began to act. Under the theory that anything was better than the near-total collapse of business and the misery of mass unemployment, he began a series of bold innovations. President Roosevelt had to drag Democratic congressmen into an acceptance of New Deal measures. Most Democratic leaders kicked and screamed in protest. And when Democratic congressmen did finally accept the New Deal, they did so less for intellectual reasons or out of a farsighted desire to help people by molding twentieth-century forces than for reasons of pure political expediency. Democratic leaders realized that President Roosevelt's ideas were popular, and they supported them simply because they wanted to be elected.

Whatever the motive of Democratic politicians, however, the innovations have become a part of our national life. There is no need to describe them in detail: public works and conservation programs, unemployment relief, the T.V.A., social security, measures to restore the solvency of, and confidence in, the nation's banks, measures to revive our prostrate farmers, the National Industrial Recovery Act, minimum wage laws, tax revisions, labor laws and labor supervision, a wide range of measures called "pump-priming," and others to regulate the business cycle and to divert resources to health, education and welfare

. . . and so on. Opposition to these innovations proved the undoing of Republican popularity.

These innovations did not work brilliantly, or even smoothly. In many cases they worked poorly; but to some degree they did work. And politically they were popular. Americans were caught up in a catastrophe they did not understand, and they accepted New Deal programs because the programs helped. More significant, perhaps, the programs seemed to say that the Democrats *wanted* to help. In their desperation, people were tired of hearing the old slogans. For millions, "rugged individualism" meant no more than waiting docilely among the army of unemployed. "Freedom of opportunity" meant little more, since lack of opportunity was equally free to all. Self-blame for their troubles made little sense, and predictions of disaster through "government intervention" had lost their power to intimidate.

And so a new era in American politics was born. A half-century of Republican predominance was ended, and in its place came a period of Democratic majorities convinced of the necessity — the rightness — of positive government action for the benefit of individual and national welfare. We are still in this period — it has lasted almost forty years.

Our Republican leaders' first reaction to positive Democratic action was hardly a reaction at all. For almost two years — 1932 to 1934 — they were too stunned and demoralized to present a meaningful opposition. The voice of Republicanism was reduced to a whisper; most Americans did not hear it at all. Quite simply, our leaders did not know how to answer the New Deal any more than they did the Depression.

When an opposition finally began to materialize, it was a potpourri of inconsistent arguments, rather than a coherent program of action. It was designed to capitalize upon discontent generated (or hopefully generated) by the New Deal, rather than to attack the national problems which inspired the New Deal. Instead of modifying a philosophy which had been obviously discredited, Republican dedication to it tended to deepen. At sea in a new political world, most Republican leaders clung frantically to an old faith — an ideology of the dangers of government action. The ideology justified itself to those who believed it; those who believed it were more convinced than ever of the rightness of their cause. But it is not too much to say that the dogmas of old Republicanism fell on the country's deaf ears. President Hoover warned Americans not to be led astray by "false gods." The false gods were in fact a return to something approaching normal national life with the help of the government, so that desperate unemployed breadwinners could feed their families. The "true gods," one learned, were a balanced budget, the gold standard and faith in laissez-faire free enterprise. And patience — to wait for the prosperity which was "just around the corner."

In the 1934 elections Republicans were reduced to a quarter of the House and Senate and a sixth of the governorships — but still Republican leaders tried to make the party a vehicle of resistance to the New Deal.

The 1936 Republican Convention in Cleveland gave itself over to attacking everything Democratic, warning of an "unconstitutional dictatorship," a "monstrous, reckless propaganda machine" and the "un-American" activities of government which had put the country "in peril." "It is nearly impossible," wrote Robert J. Donovan recently, "to imagine how a convention could have met at that point in American history and said so many things that were so meaningless to so many people." Alfred M. Landon, our 1936 presidential candidate, attacked even the immensely popular Social Security Act! Republicanism was being converted to a commitment to *opposition*. It was being reduced to criticizing, grumbling, carping about Democratic programs and their real or imagined evils — and to warning of the dangers of what this or that Democratic reform "will lead to in the future." This was negativism supreme; we were campaigning *against* the proposals of others.

Of course I do not mean to imply that all Republicans responded in the spirit of negativism. Republicanism was still a blend of several strains, one of the best of which was represented by men like Henry L. Stimson, President Hoover's Secretary of State, and later, during World War II, Secretary of War. Stimson felt that government was not "a mere organized police force, a sort of necessary evil, but rather an affirmative agency of national progress and social betterment." But voices like his were lost in the deluge of anti–New Deal rhetoric. Those Republicans who suggested that alternative programs replace opposition based on emotional slogans were largely ignored. A rigid, defensive, even regressive climate prevailed.

The result was predictable to anyone not blinded by all-pervading irrational distrust of the federal government. Alfred Landon won but two states and thirty-six per cent of the popular presidential vote. In the sixteen years since 1920 the Democratic vote for President had trebled while the Republican vote practically stood still. The great majority of voters, especially "new" voters in the cities, had been persuaded that their needs and interests were better represented by the Democratic Party.

This most unfortunate period in Republican history bears an uncomfortable resemblance to certain aspects of the present. Not in the direct sense, for Republicans are no longer, most of us, implacably opposed to the reforms of the New Deal and all that followed it. We too believe that the federal government must help attain certain goals that are deeply desired by the great mass of Americans in this age. We too agree that the nation, in the form of its government, must assume responsibility in greater or lesser measure for expanded opportunities for all citizens, of development of our cultural and natural resources and a secure and dignified old age. We believe that the rights of labor must be protected, the working man must be given an opportunity to improve his lot, the farmer must be encouraged and helped in times of disaster and that poverty, whether in pockets or spread out thinly, must be attacked.

Gradually — and not without disputes, splits, feuds and dissensions — Republicans have moved toward an acceptance of the major New Deal policies, if not in detail, at least in outline. This had to be. In the interaction between two parties, as V. O. Key has pointed out, the lot of innovation falls to one of them. Its creative measures stir dissension and embitter the minority, but as their technical and, most important, their popular success is demonstrated, as they become embedded in the system and

[87]

"consensus" of voters by continued ratification in successive elections, the minority party eventually recognizes the inevitable and accepts the new order.

This we have done: in the broadest terms, we have accepted the new order of government responsibility and action. Yet, too many of our leaders have retained too much of the spirit of negativism developed in reaction to the New Deal. They are still relegating us to the role of followers, rather than leaders. They still concentrate more on criticizing the faults of the Democrats than on analyzing the problems of the country and devising solutions of their own. Too often they behave, as an astute Republican has pointed out, like a salesman for Ford who spends most of his time expounding the faults of Chevrolet, rather than extolling the virtues of his own product. As a result, the era of Democratic predominance has prevailed to this time. It is the Democratic Party which, as the majority party, has had the primary responsibility of setting the tone of national life, establishing the goals, proposing and passing the legislation, and administering the programs. It is the Republican Party which, as the minority party, has had to offer the opposition, make the criticisms and propose alternatives and amendments to the Democratic proposals. However, it is practically impossible for a minority party which does not have the power and machinery of the federal government at its disposal to make a sustained impact on the political consciousness of the American public. Even the Republican Party's best proposals usually end up as amendments to Democratic-sponsored legislation or are incorporated in the Democratic Party legislative program and presented to the public as Democratic proposals.

The Republican Party during its years of decline has proposed a good deal of sound pioneering and remedial legislation and offered some constructive and vital amendments which have been adopted by the Democrats. (Republican contributions to Medicare and the Civil Rights Act of 1964 are but two recent examples.) But for this the Republican Party has received little or no recognition or thanks from the voters. In most instances, however, the Republican Party has been forced to react, rather than act. And this is not a comforting thought for us, who like to think of ourselves as a governing party.

Our troubles in this area have been compounded by the fact that many of the men who have carried the responsibility of Republican Party leadership have actually been out of step with the thinking of rank-and-file Republicans throughout the nation. They have said "no" even when many or most Republicans have wanted to say "yes."

A graphic demonstration of the disparity in thought and attitude between the Republican "leaders" and the Republican "led" is outlined by Herbert McClosky et al. in the June, 1960, issue of the *American Political Science Review*. Questionnaires were mailed to delegates and alternate delegates to the national party conventions asking their opinions on a number of important public-policy questions. Identical questions were asked of a sampling of Democratic and Republican voters. For the most part, the Democratic delegates and the Democratic voters shared similar views (for public ownership of natural resources — delegates 58%, voters 35%; 'for federal aid to education — delegates 66%, voters 75%; for minimum wages — delegates 50%, voters 59%; for corporate income tax — delegates 32%, voters 32%). But there was a vast gap between the thinking and response of the Republican delegates and the Republican voters (for public ownership of natural resources — delegates 13%, voters 31%; for federal aid to education — delegates 22%, voters 65%; for minimum wages — delegates 16%, voters 44%; for corporate income tax — delegates 4%, voters 23%).

Traditionally, delegates to national party conventions have been the leaders of the party, who supposedly represent the thinking of the party as a whole. But in the Republican Party there is a wide gap between the thinking of the leadership and the thinking of the membership.

Some of the wounds inflicted upon the Republican Party by the reaction of its leaders to the Depression and the New Deal have healed. But other injuries still trouble us, because we have not devoted ourselves to the active course of therapy needed to cure them. One of the most serious of these continuing injuries concerns our relationship with the nation's intellectuals. They have been consistently antagonized by some of our leaders to the point that few of them now support us. Few of them are even concerned about our fate. Under President Franklin D. Roosevelt, we alienated the intellectual community: we spoke of "woolly-minded professors," "impracticable theorists," "dupes" and "pinks" who were foolish or dangerous — or both. And in the 1950's we alienated them still further: we tolerated — some of us even encouraged — Senator Joseph R. McCarthy's senseless persecution of professors, writers and social scientists. And if the vast majority of intellectuals had despaired of our attitude before, their antagonism and antipathy to the party were strengthened under candidate Goldwater. This alienation, says Walter Lippmann, is "the root of the decline of the Republican Party." American intellectuals, who had once considered the Republican Party their natural home, flocked to the Democratic Party, giving it a capacity for dealing with issues — a capacity which we simply do not have. "The Democrats," Lippmann continues, "have pre-empted almost all of the attractive proposals because they have included so much of the intellectual community which is capable of devising attractive proposals."

Even discounting the unfortunate direct attacks upon intellectuals which many Republicans made during the years of our decline, our relations with the intellectual community have been less than cordial. No party in a complex society dealing with complex, technical issues can hope to prosper without intimate ties with intellectuals. The Democrats have maintained these ties, indeed, con-sciously sought the intellectuals out. But our ties have been tenuous at best. "Anti-intellectualism" is too strong a description of our attitude, but it is all too apparent that for many Republicans the universities and research cen-ters are a kind of alien, even hostile, territory.

"Perhaps this resistance to the intellectual is in the proc-ess of being gradually overcome," Malcolm Moos has written, "but there is more than a grain of truth to the as-sertion that a large part of the leadership of the Republi-can Party is anti-intellectual to the point of keeping out of its councils valuable human resources of men and women not only dedicated to the Republican Party but often in key positions to keep a dynamic interest in Re-publicanism alive in the nation's intellectual centers."

Most of the nation's "thinkers" respond to our suspi-

[91]

cion of them with a corresponding suspicion of us. There are exceptions, of course, but few. Few intellectuals find themselves comfortable among us, not only because they resent the "anti-egghead" undercurrent in the party, but principally because they cannot work fruitfully in a climate of dogmatic incantation of oversimplified platitudes, a climate in which meaningful discussion of complex issues is nearly impossible. By the nature of things, intellectuals are usually in the vanguard of social and economic thought, working with new ideas and new solutions. Their seemingly unorthodox proposals often become truisms in a decade. Yet too many Republican leaders have been too quick to dismiss new ideas as unworkable, whatever their merits. Too many seem to respect clichés and distrust ideas. They are, for example, likely to say to social scientists, who are seriously grappling with the causes of crime, that Republicans do not approve of spending money on that problem because the Republican Party stands against "government intervention" and for "the sanctity of the individual and the American way of life." Such platitudes have driven the intellectuals from our ranks.

NINE

✤ ✤ ✤

Slogans without Solutions

O F all the unfortunate developments encouraged by
Republican leaders in their reaction to the New
Deal, none was more harmful than the tendency to
counter Democratic proposals with slogans, generalities
and platitudes. Now as then (although now much less
than then) our leaders are apt to laden their speeches
and press conferences with ringing allusions to "freedom,"
"liberty," the "example of our forefathers," the "traditional
values of the American system" — without explaining
how they should be applied to present-day problems.

Flag-waving and slogan-making do have value to the
country. They supply a certain pomp and sense of continuity — that feeling of pride in country which tingles
the spine and helps hold America together. For Americans
lacking as they do a ceremonial head of state, like a king or
queen, to whom to direct their emotional attachment to
country and tradition, reference to the American values is
both necessary and good.

Necessary and good, that is, within certain limitations.
Politicians tend to exceed those limitations. But Republi-

can politicians, being in the minority, can least afford that
luxury.

To "reman the bastions of liberty" is not a program, but
a slogan; it may warm the hearts of people attending a
campaign rally, but it cannot help them solve their problems. It does not "stick to the ribs" of most voters long
enough to accompany them to the voting booths. The abstractions of liberty, justice, freedom for all; of thrift, individual enterprise, and the prevention of government dictatorship are great goods in themselves. But they can also
become retreats from dealing with real issues, retreats in
which stale minds and timid spirits take refuge.

I first became aware of the futility of campaign-by-
slogan in my earliest venture into politics, as a candidate,
in 1950 and 1952, for state representative from Boston's
Ward 12. The ward was in a residential, largely middle
and lower-middle class section of the city; and parts of it
were beginning to be settled by low-income Negroes. It
had many of the problems which face most of our great
urban centers: inadequate transportation and understaffed schools; housing which was deteriorating into
slums; problems of declining business activity, unemployment, irregular garbage collection, substandard street
lighting and recreation, increasing delinquency and
crime; an approaching incipient Negro ghetto with all
that that implies. I walked through the ward, trying to
study its problems. The people wanted to shake hands
and banter, but they were also deeply concerned with
the real issues facing them.

Republican candidates for higher office came into the
ward both in person and through the media of radio and
television. They talked movingly about the "free-

enterprise system," "Washington bureaucracy," the "sanctity of the individual," and the "danger of creeping socialism." They made references to the traditional virtues of sound government, low taxes, a balanced budget, and to What Made America Great. I observed that the people of Ward 12 were less than excited by the repetition of the old platitudes and old warnings, but would have been deeply impressed with concrete solutions to tangible issues. References to the splendid success of individual enterprise and of the free-enterprise system, however stirring themselves, simply could not help the people of Ward 12 solve their community problems. I think Republican candidates who have faced similar situations know what I mean. Slogans without meaningful programs are hardly sufficient ammunition to do battle against the Democratic opposition.

The trouble with political slogans is that many of them are meaningless or misleading — and are recognized as such by the majority of voters. They may in fact achieve an effect opposite from the one desired. Slogans often win cheers from supporters and convince a candidate of his oratorical prowess. But in the long run, they cause the skeptical and uncommitted to believe that the candidate is barren of ideas. Most voters are quite perceptive about political speeches, quite capable of separating campaign rhetoric from real answers to real problems. However fervently delivered, vague speeches about "American ideals," "American virtues," and "American greatness" remain unconvincing as long as they remain vague.

Consider, for example, the set of slogans which exhort us to "preserve and protect our individual freedoms." Preserving and protecting freedom is a noble pursuit; everyone wants his freedom secured. The question is, how? Whose freedom are we talking about? What do the majority of Americans mean by "freedom"? Which "individuals" do we have in mind? Are we thinking about these concepts in terms of the majority's environment and experiences, or our own preconceptions? This slogan is usually used — together with many others about "reckless government spending" and "Washington control" — to oppose new governmental programs. But does a program to grant federal scholarships to needy college students, for example, in fact narrow our freedom or extend it? Or a program to provide federal aid for slum clearance or for elimination of poverty pockets? From the point of view of voters, are these onerous limitations on personal liberties or welcomed expansion of the democratic ideal?

No doubt these programs do limit freedom in one sense; they presuppose an expansion of government activity with all the paperwork, bureaucracy, surveys and supervision that that implies. But is there not also a vast increase in freedom for students and slum-dwellers? Do not these programs on balance expand our freedoms — the freedoms of opportunity, education, and of individual and national progress? Do they not really represent growth of American greatness and American ideals?

The great shortcoming of slogans about "the freedom of the individual" is that they invariably deal with but a single aspect of freedom. Most voters, however, do not think of freedom simply as an absence of restrictions or of government activity — not simply as being free *from* something. It is also being free *for* something. To oppose anti-poverty, education, beautification, and urban rehabilitation programs undertaken by the federal government on the grounds that they limit freedom is to open oneself to a charge of a narrow-mindedness or callousness. It is a reflection of the doctrine that Americans' primary concern is protecting themselves against the evil designs of Washington bureaucrats — a doctrine that is simply not supported by facts.

Or consider the problem of medical care for the aged, or the more complex problem of mental health. Does an American who becomes ill think first of freedom *from* "government interference" in these areas, or freedom *for* access to adequate medical care and the advantages of current research? To those who have dealt with these problems, I think the answer is obvious. Whatever the theoretical merits of these two interpretations of freedom, in practical terms the positive approach is more popular. And more important, it is in keeping with enlightened and civilized government.

Many Republican candidates have used slogans suggesting that "America is in peril" because the "planners of the welfare system" are dedicated to "subjugating the freedom of the individual to the interests of the state." "The rights of the individual are being undermined!" "Let us reman the citadels of liberty!" "The welfare state is the halfway point on the march to end freedom!" But at best they are using one-sided interpretations of freedom and individual rights. For it is precisely the individual that welfare programs are designed to protect — the individual with problems, with children to educate, elderly parents who require frequent medical care, a family to protect against the dangers of spreading slums.

Republicans can justifiably criticize the concept or operation of specific programs. And here, I think, there is much to criticize. But merely to oppose welfare programs with slogans about the "freedom of the individual" is to misinterpret the American concept of freedom. For most Americans, freedom means a chance to move onward and upward, to improve their living standards in the broadest sense. Abstract talk about the "erosion of traditional freedoms" competes quite unfavorably with specific programs designed to provide specific remedies for specific problems in our national life.

There are those who believe the old slogans; in some quarters they still make a deep emotional impression. It is also true that most Americans are disturbed by the growth of the federal government. Most of us have a vague feeling of uneasiness about the expansion of government activity in many areas of our lives. But most of us, I also believe, have a greater fear of what might happen were government to withdraw from many areas of our national life. To interpret "freedom," "Americanism," "individualism" as a state of nature in which each man must somehow secure his own health, education and welfare is to misinterpret the needs and wants of the American people. A few voters still feel that way — but not enough to win one election in ten. We must not be deluded by uneasiness about the expansion of government services. The uneasiness about the alternative — shrinking of government services — is even greater.

Let us not be deluded either by the nature of the uneasiness about big government. In fact, much of it is uneasiness not merely about bigness of government, but about bigness in general — in our commerce, our means of communication, our unions, everything in our society. Enormous concentrations of corporate economic power,

[98]

in some cases greater than that of many foreign governments, have developed in our country. These immense corporations have great power over our lives — our jobs, our
pensions, our culture, our standards of taste and the use of
America's resources. The ordinary American is apt to regard government not as a threat, but as a countervailing
power that protects individual interests in the world of
bigness.

I believe it is a grave mistake to attribute the individual's frustrations in our complex industrialized society solely
to the restrictions imposed by government. Much more
severe restrictions are imposed by the nature of industrialized society itself, and more often than not, government
"intervenes" to correct abuses and solve problems which
could not successfully be attacked either by individuals
alone or by corporations or unions. It is illogical to assume that big government means enslavement while big
business and big labor mean freedom. Yet this myth and
the one-sided interpretation of freedom it implies continues to be endorsed by too many Republicans.

But of all the myths propagated in the last decades,
none is more fanciful than the myth that the federal government is destroying the American character and bringing disaster to the American economic system. Since
1932, many Republican leaders have been opposing Democratic proposals with predictions of ugly and frightful
consequences, few of which have materialized. "The end
of the American Dream!" "The road to socialism!" "The destruction of the American economy!" "The extinction of
freedom!" "The downfall of business and abandonment
of the American way!" "Disaster! Chaos! Dictatorship!

Ruin!" I need not recount the long, sad history of those soothsayers and their predictions of disaster. Many of the most prominent Republican leaders said that social security and unemployment compensation represented the beginning of the end of everything good in America, if not the end of America itself. These innovations were called hair-brained and utopian, ruthless and tyrannical. They were going to enslave us as servants of a bankrupt state. If the New Deal (which President Hoover called "the most stupendous invasion of the whole spirit of Liberty that the nation has witnessed since the days of Colonial America") were made permanent, "America would cease to be American."

Voters remember Republican predictions of disaster made early in the New Deal partly because they are repeated today. The language is far more moderate; few Republicans now talk of "criminal" or "power-mad" Washington bureaucrats. But some trot out the "power-hungry" slogans and a host of others similar in spirit. They still talk about the perils and sinfulness of deficit spending even though it has harmed no one in three decades because, as economists tell us, governments, like corporations, often should borrow money in order to operate in a businesslike fashion. They still lament the "crushing burden of debt" and the "day when our orgies of spending will ruin our children or our children's children" — even though history has proved these predictions unfounded. They still warn, at almost each new proposal for government action, about the catastrophic effects on business initiative and profits — even though corporate profits are far higher now (a few giant corporations are netting nearly two billion dollars in profits annually) than the most visionary businessmen dreamed they might be thirty years ago. They still speak of the trend toward "socialism" and the "beginning of the end of the free-enterprise system," even though free enterprise, particularly in the form of our great industrial corporations, is more prosperous and self-confident — and more securely protected against failure — than ever before in the world's history. They still warn about the "sapping of America's greatness," the "loss of our traditional sources of strength," and the "deterioration of our national grandeur," even though America has become, in this century, by far the richest and most powerful nation on earth. They still couch their opposition to new programs in terms of the incalculable damage the programs will wreak upon our society, even though program after program which they had opposed in similar terms in the past has turned out to be salutary, not damaging — a fact that they have had to recognize sheepishly within a few years after its adoption. They still speak the language of gloom, pessimism and impending ruin.

And what effect have these alarmist's slogans had upon the voters? The effect has been what one would suppose: a general discrediting of all Republican candidates. Voters are not without powers of observation and not without memories. When voters have heard grave warnings about the evaporation of investment and profits, about the destruction of their liberty, property, and sense of well-being, and discover that the opposite is taking place, they tend to ignore the forecaster along with the forecast.

Too many Republicans have cried "wolf" too long and too often. The catastrophes have not materialized, America has not been ruined, nor has America become un-

American. "When you put the old slogans to bed and start talking seriously," many Independent voters have told me, "many of us will be willing to listen and willing to join."

I might go on about the legacy of negativism and slogan-making inherited from the 1930's, but I trust I have made my point. The climate that discourages intellectuals from serving the Republican Party also discourages the majority of city-dwellers and wage-earners from feeling a sense of identification with Republicanism. We are caught in a vicious cycle; intellectuals tend to avoid the party because it discourages creative approaches for specific problems which interest them; and because they avoid the party, the party is less and less equipped to offer new solutions. As we fail to offer new solutions to social problems, our base of support shrinks; and as our support shrinks, excluding divergent interests, our outlook becomes more and more narrow and rigid. These are both symptoms and causes of a serious malady.

What is taking place, slowly, is the consolidation of a single spirit of "orthodox" Republicanism and an elimination of elements which do not fit that orthodoxy. In a nation composed of scores of divergent, conflicting interests, this is an incapacitating affliction. We are steadily eliminating interests that are unhappy with the orthodoxy — and along with them, any real chance for winning consistent victories.

We are talking to ourselves, lecturing for our own satisfaction. The applause at election rallies seems as loud as ever, but in fact fewer Independents, Democrats and even Republicans are applauding. We are encouraging a wild enthusiasm among a segment of our supporters, but driving a larger segment — as well as millions of potential supporters — away. Fewer and fewer Americans take us seriously as a party equipped to govern contemporary America.

This is not to say that Democratic leaders are not guilty of resorting to slogans too. They have more than their share of tired platitudes and empty abstractions, and many of them no less meaningless and misleading than ours. Many of them annoy the intelligent voter with their promises of all things to all men. The Democrats are masters of the salesman's pitch, the political platitude and the campaign slogan. But they have demonstrated the art of mixing slogans with solutions, or at least what passes for solutions.

Our reliance on slogans, on the other hand, reduces us to political impotence; it relegates us to debate and dissent — to speeches, press conferences, *words* — while giving the Democrats a clear field for action. While our leaders are talking of "our political heritage," "traditional American values" and "preserving the freedom of the individual," Democratic leaders are pitching their appeal to specific needs of specific people.

The results are predictable. Public housing is built, aid to education is administered, health-insurance plans are devised, antipoverty and urban-renewal programs are established — and all with a minimum of ideas and participation from Republican leaders. For up to the eleventh hour before adoption, we had been arguing not how the plans and programs should be devised, but whether they should exist at all.

It is true that some programs are planned and executed with *some* Republican participation, adding or adjusting items in accordance with our special knowledge. And at the last moment, a few minor concessions are usually made to satisfy some of our justifiable complaints. But our real talents are sparsely used: our imagination as politicians, our skills as lawmakers, our experience as administrators are barely tapped.

I am suggesting that reliance on slogans has kept us from a meaningful competition for the acceptance of specific proposals, and that we have imposed this restriction on ourselves. Only by talking issues instead of slogans can we remove it and compete on equal terms.

These symptoms are the heritage of the New Deal era. There is a chasm between what Republicans have been saying and what most voters feel is important. We have not been able to adjust our thinking to that of the majority of the American people. Slogans, platitudes and generalities cannot bridge the gap. Nor will appeals to party unity or intensified criticism of the Democrats or renewed dedication to the Republican past. For all of these approaches are defensive. They draw us inward upon ourselves instead of outward upon the nation and its problems. They are reflections of negativism which were developed as a reaction to the New Deal and which have nothing in common with the early tradition of the Republican Party.

The World during the Republican
Decline

I MUST now backtrack to the early 1930's. We have been
asking, what has happened to America during the years
of Republican decline? But it is equally important to in-
quire about the changes that have come upon the rest of
the world, and upon America's relationship to the world
during that period.

The reaction of leading Republicans to America's participation in the League of Nations antedates our decline.
But it should be mentioned briefly because the attitudes
which crystallized in opposition to the League remained
the attitudes of Republican leadership for many succeeding years. And to a certain extent, they remain the attitudes
of Republican leadership today.

Republican opposition to the Versailles Peace Treaty,
which included American membership in the League,
did not lose the party many votes, for the country was
then tired of the international involvement thrust upon it
by World War I and eager to forget Europe and its troubles. But the opposition was symbolic of the party's tend-

ency to miss splendid opportunities, both for guiding the country boldly toward its destiny in foreign affairs and for reaping the political rewards of positive, imaginative leadership.

For, until the time when anti-League Republicans managed to dominate the party, Republicans had been known as the proponents and executors of internationalism. With few exceptions, Republicans were America's men of vision, competence and experience in foreign affairs. Most Democrats reflected narrow, sectional interests that viewed all foreign involvements with suspicion based largely on ignorance of international affairs. Until the rejection of the League, it was the Republicans — diplomats, professors, elder statesmen, directors of industry and finance — who were known and trusted in the capitals of Europe as the natural leaders of an enlightened American foreign policy. It was the Republicans who recognized that we could no longer lose ourselves on our own frontier and ignore the rest of the world.

Indeed, the very concept of an association of nations to keep the peace was originally a Republican idea! It was conceived by a group of farsighted Republican internationalists who were convinced that America would have to play a leading role in establishing a rational, workable world order. Later, however, it was opposed by most leading Republicans largely for reasons of temporary political expediency. Since President Woodrow Wilson championed the League, "smart" politics — it was assumed — dictated that Republicans oppose it, if only to tarnish President Wilson's record. It was also assumed that great political capital could be made by warning the country of the League's potential evils and dangers. This was an unfortunate decision because, although it *did* temporarily discredit President Wilson, in the long run it discredited the Republican Party more. It started the party on a long descent into isolationism, just at the time when the opposite — a forceful, purposeful internationalism — was required.

Actually, it could be argued that this period antedated the time when intelligent internationalism was needed in the conduct of our foreign policy. For the 1920's and the first half of the 1930's was a period when most nations, and America most of all, turned their backs on the rest of the world. There was little to distinguish between the attitude of the Republican and Democratic parties on foreign affairs in that period, and little in their policies which distinguished either of them. But nevertheless the seeds of Republican difficulty were being sown. On the one great foreign policy issue of the time — tariffs — most Republican leaders sided with the past rather than the future, helping build barriers between America and the rest of the world. Republican congressmen were nearly unanimous in support of ever higher tariffs. A pinnacle was reached in 1930 with the passage of the Smoot-Hawley Act, which has been called the "modern version of the 'Tariff of Abominations.'"

Meanwhile, as Republicans helped encourage a retreat into isolationism, great twentieth-century forces were developing that were to make isolation impossible. The 1930's witnessed as vast a change in the forces which shape world politics as any other in history. A technological revolution was making all men neighbors. Marvelous new inventions were shrinking the world to a fraction of its former size in terms of time and convenience of communication and travel. And marvelous — or ghastly — military techniques were multiplying by hundreds of times the destructive ability of armies and the ability to transport destruction. Willy-nilly, the peoples of the world were being drawn together into a common fate; there was less and less opportunity to "go it alone." The appalling twentieth-century totalitarianisms were being spawned — Fascism in Italy and Germany, and Bolshevism in Russia. And although they seemed safely distant and appeared to confirm the notion that America had best keep to herself, avoiding the messiness and ugliness of foreign entanglements, in fact the emergence of these dictatorships proved (or ought to have proved) the opposite. For ours was already one world, as Wendell Willkie emphasized later. What happened anywhere had inescapable consequences for America. And here lay the most important change in America's relationship to the world, and perhaps in the world itself: we were now a major power, potentially *the* major power. We were the richest, most powerful industrial and military nation. Our very blessings of wealth, location and human energy inevitably thrust upon us a natural leadership role. Sooner or later, American statesmen would be forced to recognize that reality and to accept the responsibilities of a foreign policy corresponding to our stature and strength. The Japanese invasion of Manchuria, the Italian invasion of Ethiopia, the German invasion of Poland, the Soviet invasion of Finland *were* our business. The invasions were attempted, and succeeded, partly because America made clear to the world that she was not concerned.

Democratic leaders were slow to recognize the significance of these changes in the world and of America's place in the world. They hesitated and procrastinated throughout the 1930's. They justified this inaction by saying that the American people were deeply isolationist, but this was a lame excuse. As the officials responsible for national security, they owed the country candid information about the realities of world politics and the dangers to America of militaristic aggression in Europe and Asia. But the painful truth is that when Democratic leaders finally did awaken to their responsibilities, most Republican leaders tried to convince the nation that all responsibility should be avoided. They countered President Franklin D. Roosevelt's proposals to help our future allies with their own formula for the easy way out: to pretend that German and Japanese aggression did not exist, or if it did exist, it was not a threat to world peace or American security.

The Republican voting record in Congress on the eve of Pearl Harbor was probably our greatest failing in this century. In 1939, after Hitler's rape of Europe and Japan's thrust into the Asian mainland had already begun, all seven Republican senators on the Foreign Relations Committee voted not to allow the Allies to purchase arms from America. The next year, congressional Republicans voted two to one against the Selective Service Act; in 1941, four to one against the Lend-Lease agreements, and again in 1941 — the year of our entry into the war — five to one against the extension of Selective Service! A few farsighted Republican internationalists such as Henry L. Stimson and William Allen White, the prescient Kansas newspaperman, were among the first Americans to recognize the dangers of Japanese and Nazi aggression. But most Republican leaders in and out of the Congress clung to the notion that these "distant" matters did not concern us. (President Hoover, presidential candidate Landon, and Senator Robert A. Taft all opposed Lend-Lease. And when Wendell Willkie spoke in favor of it, he was excoriated by a large group of Republican leaders.) Unfortunately, our leaders did not help efforts to prepare America to accept the realities of world politics and to accept its inevitable duty in World War II. The theory was advanced that Democrats were exaggerating the perils of the international situation to gain political advantage — that President Roosevelt's plan for a dictatorship (to be established by stirring up fear of war) was more dangerous than the Axis dictatorships themselves.

Not all Republicans were isolationist, and not all isolationists were Republicans, but the party's congressional leaders stood almost unanimously against deeper involvement in foreign affairs. The abdication of national leadership; the opportunism of clinging to isolationism, the narrow partisanship of attacking President Roosevelt as a "warmonger," the failure to understand the threat of totalitarianism to the entire world, the willingness to let Europe and Asia "stew in their own juice" — these attitudes hurt the Republican Party severely on the eve of the Second World War. For the world had reached the point where all of us stewed in the same juice.

I refer to this period of Republican history not because the party has clung to its pre-World War II isolationism. For the most part, the fond belief that America could be kept free and safe by keeping the country quarantined from the infections of other nations had disappeared by the middle of World War II. Many of the most determined Republican isolationists failed to be reelected, and most of those who were reelected quietly discarded their old dogmatism. Senator Arthur Vandenburg of Michigan was a classic example of this Republican transformation. He began his senatorial career as a dogged isolationist, but ended it as an enlightened internationalist. His work and leadership were essential in establishing the Truman Doctrine, the Marshall Plan, and the Atlantic Alliance as the foundation of our postwar foreign policy.

Isolationism has long been buried as the spirit of the party. Even if a few Republican senators did seem eager to return to it after World War II (the only two "nay" votes on the Senate confirmation of American entry into the United Nations were Republican, as were eleven of the thirteen votes against the North Atlantic Treaty), the great majority of Republican leaders have reached an awareness of America's natural role as a great world power and the obligations which accompany that role. Happily, isolationism is one dogma we have buried. And we have replaced it with a sober recognition of the responsibilities of world leadership.

Nor have I referred to isolationism because our relatively short romance with it continues to hurt us at the polls. Perhaps a few American families still vote against us because of the lack of perception of many of our leaders about the forces leading to World War II. But I think their number is small. We were wrong, but we admitted our mistake, at least tacitly, and we corrected it. Americans rarely bear a grudge against a political party for that kind of error. And considering the Republican Party's contribution to America's foreign policy in earlier periods, this mistake indeed deserves to be excused.

But I think many of our party leaders have only half

learned the lessons of our isolationist experience. After World War II, vast new changes broke upon the world, bringing America into a new phase of foreign relations and faced with new global problems. The rise of the Communist threat to America and the non-Communist world appeared, superficially, to parallel the rise of fascism. Having learned the perils of noninvolvement (perils both to the nation and the Republican Party), most prominent Republican leaders responded to the challenge of the Communist threat by supporting the vast American commitment to thwart and contain it by military means. But, in fact, the Communist threat is essentially different from the threat of the Axis powers in World War II. The earlier threat was direct: it took the form of overt military aggression. The present threat is largely indirect: it takes many forms, but concentrates primarily on subversion, the cultivation of mass support, on "boring from within."

For the changes that have come upon the post-World War II world are essentially different from those of any other era. An unparalleled surge of nationalism and anticolonialism has led to the emergence of literally scores of new nations containing hundreds of millions of people who were formerly subject to colonial rule. This era marks the collapse of Western empires and the rise of new nations with hungry populations, great aspirations, and little economic development or experience at self-government. These great postwar changes were bound to take place sooner or later. For historical forces were operating everywhere in the world, stimulating the desire for national independence, democracy, and an end to oppression. But World War II gave these forces a great push forward: after the independence of India was proclaimed in 1947, the rush of the formation of new nations had begun.

The new nations, as well as many older, former colonial nations in Asia, Africa and Latin America are economically underdeveloped and present American foreign policy with a whole series of new problems, not just the single problem of stopping Communism. The solutions to these problems require those qualities of knowledge and imagination, courage and statesmanship which we Republicans sacrificed during our isolationist experience.

America needs these qualities now more than ever, for if the perils of this era are less dramatic than those of World War II, our responsibility as a world leader has become far greater. As in the days of the rise of Hitler, a few Republican leaders are still inclined to believe that discontent in obscure lands is none of America's business — and they are disinclined to investigate the real causes of that discontent. Another splendid opportunity awaits us to improve our fortune and that of the nation by exercising imaginative, farsighted leadership in foreign affairs. And we must seize this opportunity.

ELEVEN

✤ ✤ ✤

Attaining Victory while Retaining
Principles

I N a sense political campaigns are like military wars.
When one acquaints himself with the hardships, frightful blunders, wrong guesses, lack of supplies, and the bad
luck and bad weather which plagued the victorious army,
he is at a loss to understand how that army in fact managed to win. That becomes clear only after a study of the
defeated army. For the hardships, blunders, wrong
guesses, lack of supplies and bad luck are inevitably worse
on the other side. Our own war with the Democrats falls
into this pattern.

"The Democrats have made so many blunders, revealed
such corruption and disunity, and operated on so low a
political plane that defeat seemed inevitable," Samuel Lubell has written. "But the Republican Party has managed, by hard work in the wrong direction, to overcome
this handicap and prove itself more disunited, more capable of blunders, so that it has won the race to the precipice
of defeat — almost oblivion."

If this and all I have written in previous chapters

[114]

sound harsh, I urge us to look once more at the facts, which are harsher. Harsh facts require harsh criticism, especially when the sufferer is a victim of his own mistakes, repeated consistently after ample warning. We like to think that Republicans look dispassionately at the facts, judge people by their performances, and speak out unflinchingly about failure when unflinching talk is required. We do not admire incompetence and excuses in others; we should not — at the very least, to avoid looking foolishly hypocritical — tolerate them in ourselves.

The facts, to touch upon them briefly once more, are grim. Twenty-seven per cent of American voters identified themselves with the Republican Party in 1952; in 1956 the figure had inched up to twenty-nine per cent; in 1960 it returned to twenty-seven per cent, and in 1964 it fell to twenty-four per cent. Now two Americans consider themselves Democrats for every one who regards himself a Republican. (More precisely, according to Dr. Gallup, there are fifty-three Democrats for every twenty-five Republicans.)

We might be proud of this figure — if America operated under a multi-party system. After all, the allegiance of a quarter of all eligible voters is something to be taken seriously. Many Western European parties would rejoice if they could win support of that magnitude. Twenty-seven million voters for a Republican presidential candidate is an impressive figure too — a dramatic figure, if one ignores the forty-three million Americans who voted against us. Little satisfaction can be eked from our own "successes" if the opposition has vastly more. One cannot reasonably talk of success in a two-party system unless one talks in terms of majorities. A minority party that congratulates itself on its performance is practicing a form of self-delusion.

I would feel uneasy about speaking of such elementary, self-evident matters were it not for the fact that they seem to escape many Republicans, or at least to be relegated to the far edge of consciousness, shunted aside by impassioned talk of our great past, our few victories and our hopes for the future. In some Republican quarters, the myth is being assiduously developed that the party leaders, like the German generals in World War I, never really suffered defeat.

Twenty-seven million Americans may not be wrong, but we are grievously wrong to take satisfaction in that number. What about majorities? What about *winning?* What about talking of the underlying trends in American voting habits, instead of the exceptions to those trends?

During the decade and a half I referred to above, the period of my own active participation in politics, the percentage of American voters identifying themselves as Democrats has increased from slightly less to slightly more than *twice* the Republican figure. Even conceding that the election figures are less drastic than these (because a smaller percentage of Americans identifying themselves as Democratic actually vote than those who consider themselves Republicans), the Republican minority has become so narrow that almost every election is an uphill battle. Outside of our old party strongholds, we have been winning electoral victories only when favored by extraordinary circumstances.

Fortunately, American politics are flexible enough to provide extraordinary circumstances with some degree of frequency. Glamorous personalities — military heroes, former film stars and other celebrities — win victories from time to time, and even though they are primarily personal victories, some slight advantage usually does accrue to the Republican Party in which, more often than not, the celebrities have become active shortly before their election. Or other fortuitous circumstances — Democratic mistakes, blunders, corruption, or simply a desire to "turn the rascals out" after long, easy years in office — produce defeats here and there. And good luck and good candidates (for we often do offer superior candidates) help us win a share, if not "our share," of majorities in individual elections. In all but these unusual circumstances, however, in all but the safe districts, the label "Republican" is considered by many to be a severe handicap. Many Republicans secretly hope that the turnout on election day will be small, for the fewer the number of registered voters voting their party preferences, the greater the Republican chances. In the nation and most states, Republican candidates must win practically the entire Republican vote, almost all of the Independent vote, and a good portion of the Democratic vote in order to be elected. This presents Republican candidates with an almost intolerable burden.

The Republican dilemma is reflected in the campaign hazards of some of the party's most attractive and able candidates, men who are often mentioned as potential presidential nominees. In several populous cities and states where Republicans have recently run for mayor, senator and governor, many have elected to drastically underplay — even totally abandon — their party label. The candidate considers that he has no choice. He believes that a Republican simply *cannot* win by associating himself with the party record. This is a sad spectacle, but one for which the Republican Party must share the blame.

In my three campaigns for statewide office, I have stood as a Republican, spoken as a Republican, and prominently displayed the Republican label in all my campaign materials. And I believe that all Republican candidates *should* campaign as Republicans. If a candidate accepts his party nomination, he should accept all of the responsibilities of that nomination. As a matter of fact, the voter is not fooled by a candidate's refusal to use his party's label. Ultimately, the voter sees the party designation, on the ballot or voting machine if nowhere else.

Attractive Republican candidates — and particularly those who have potential appeal in populous industrial states and major cities — are undermining the party's strength by "going it alone," avoiding the party label. These candidates are Republicans. They represent the party as much as any other candidates. They have as much right — indeed, as much obligation — to define "Republicanism" as candidates from less populous areas. If voters across the nation do not identify the Republican Party with these attractive, dynamic Republican leaders, the party will never grow and prosper. If these candidates avoid the party label and shirk their party responsibilities during election campaigns, at the very time when their identification with Republicanism would be most beneficial to the party as a whole, the shaping of the party will be left to other candidates who, too often, are unable to communicate with the masses of urban voters. And so we have another vicious cycle: to most voters in the crucial, populous states, the Republican Party seems unable to represent their interests — and the Republican candidates most able to change this image feel they cannot risk the attempt.

Yet I do understand and sympathize with the plight of Republican candidates who, after looking at comparative party enrollment figures and recent election returns, decide to campaign without the Republican label. It seems to me that it would be far more useful for Republicans to criticize not those Republican candidates who disassociate themselves from the party during difficult elections, but the deficiencies of the party which compel those candidates to take that action.

It is time to confront a troublesome question that recurs periodically in the analysis of American politics. Why don't all "liberals" join the Democratic Party and all "conservatives" the Republican Party? Why don't we stand up honestly and be counted in our "natural homes" — and at the same time bring a semblance of order to our chaotic body politic?

The merits of this notion have been debated endlessly by American political scientists. Those who favor it argue that only cohesive parties, whose members are committed to a common outlook and a common set of goals, are able to pursue their programs effectively and bear the responsibility — for action both taken and not taken — of purposeful government and opposition. There is no hope for vigorous, effective politics, say these scholars, as long as points of view in each party are scrambled into a meaningless maze, with a Republican senator, Jacob Javits, working at cross-purposes with a Republican senator, Strom Thurmond, and a Democratic senator, Wayne

Morse, hardly able to agree on the simplest issue with a Democratic senator, Harry Byrd. Why not put the Javits's and the Morse's, and the Thurmond's and the Byrd's together where they belong and end the internal bickering that reduces the sense of common purpose in each party?

Other scholars, however, disagree. Those who argue against the notion of regrouping the two wings of each party and realigning the thrust of American politics point out that the nation is composed not of two opposing political camps, "liberal" and "conservative," but of hundreds of shifting minorities which group one way on one issue and another way on the next. The unwritten laws of American politics demand that the parties overlap substantially in principle, policy, character, appeal and purpose, or cease to be parties with any hope of winning a national election. Far from being a disruptive influence, these analysts conclude, our major parties provide cohesion, stability, and responsibility in American politics. For they must appeal to broad coalitions of regional, occupational, religious and other interests — coalitions broad enough to win national elections. And the compromise achieved by thrashing out issues within both parties is essential to the smooth operation of the two-party system.

I can add nothing new to this venerable debate. Both sides make strong points; one can select those he likes to support his own views. But this issue should not be argued in theoretical terms alone. One must try to analyze the consequences of a liberal-conservative party cleavage in terms of practical politics.

The first of these consequences would be, I think, a "dreadful calamity" (as Theodore Roosevelt put it) for the nation, and I think permanent disaster for the Republican Party. In 1950, Governor Thomas E. Dewey made a classic prediction of what was likely to happen were our parties to be sharply divided on the basis of interest and doctrine. "These impractical theorists . . . want to drive all moderates and liberals out of the Republican Party and have the remainder join forces with the conservative groups in the South. Then they would have everything neatly arranged indeed. The Democratic Party would be the liberal-to-radical party. The Republican Party would be the conservative-to-reactionary party. The results would be neatly arranged, too. The Republicans would lose every election and the Democrats would win every election."

No one can be sure of course that this hypothesis is accurate. But the election of 1964, the closest we have had to a laboratory test, seems to confirm it beyond a reasonable doubt. It was as striking a proof as I hope we shall ever see.

No one can be sure either that perpetual minority status for the Republican Party would cause deep, or even superficial, damage to the well-being of our political system. But this is an assumption I think we all make: a rough balance of power and influence with both parties given a real chance of victory at most elections is the *sine qua non* for a vigorous two-party system. "What serves a political party ill serves democracy, and hence all of us, the same."

But even were this not the case, even if a "conservative-to-reactionary" Republican Party were able to stand its ground in most elections, I believe that a party split based solely on economic interest and ideological doctrine would be disastrous for the nation.

We hear a great deal about the "classlessness" of American society. Surely this is overdrawn; surely we do have something approximating classes, as every society must. Still, in comparison to other societies in the world, both contemporary and ancient, America is remarkably classless. Class lines are blurred; class interests are diverse, and there is enough opportunity to advance to a higher class, even the highest class, to justify emphasizing America's class mobility, rather than its rigidity. We are not classless, but we act as if we were, which in many ways has the same effect.

It might be said, in other words, that America's classlessness is a myth. But like all myths, this one helped shape reality in its image.

Both the myth and the reality it reflects would crumble were our parties to be organized along distinct liberal-conservative lines — which would mean, inevitably, along class lines. Class barriers would harden; antagonism sharpen; political debate would grow "cleaner" but also more bitter. Free of competing groups which force both parties to make internal compromises, both parties would indeed be able to present the voters with clear-cut alternatives and a coherent set of candidates and ideologies. But this would introduce a tragically divisive atmosphere into American politics.

Intraparty compromise is the glue that holds our parties and our political system together. Once dissolved, there is no guarantee that something will appear to replace it. Nor is there a guarantee that parties based on a liberal-conservative split would not split further. Once organized along class lines, our parties might splinter into small, tightly organized factions representing distinct economic interests as in some European countries. One can picture the divisive tone such a development would bring to American politics.

European observers often suggest that a more divisive tone is precisely what we need. But few European observers are able to perceive and understand the unique flavor of American politics, with its healthy atmosphere of compromise and tolerance. Because of its size, regional and economic diversity and federal organization, America is composed of an unusual number of divergent, competing interests. Loose-jointed parties able to appeal to divergent interests are essential therefore to sustain our atmosphere of compromise and tolerance. "No America without democracy, no democracy without politics, no politics without parties, no parties without compromise and moderation," Clinton Rossiter has said.

No simple conclusion can be reached about so complex a question as why all liberals do not join the Democratic Party and all conservatives, the Republican. I think it can be fairly said that rearranging our parties to represent class interests and doctrinaire ideologies would constitute a cure more dangerous than the ailment. "We would do well to cherish our present parties," Professor Rossiter has written, "and work only gingerly for their improvement."

I have been arguing that the Republican Party's failure has been demonstrated repeatedly, consistently, unmistakably in electoral and public opinion polls. And that the majority of Americans have been rejecting contemporary Republicanism, or what it believes to be contemporary Republicanism, for thirty-five years. I have been saying that many Republican leaders have not understood the needs of the times. But what if I am wrong? What if those leaders have a greater understanding of fundamental American values than do I? What if the majority of the voters is wrong?

Surely if the majority *is* wrong — as majorities often are — we cannot fairly be accused of failure. To defend a set of valid principles is not failure. No matter how unpopular the principles. I have been supporting my criticism with evidence of electoral losses. But is it important to win when winning requires a sacrifice of principle? When winning requires us to do wrong? Are we to run up a flag on a weathervane to see which way the political winds are blowing before taking our stands on current issues? Are we to operate on the basis of sheer opportunism — to sample the majority's mood with public opinion polls and fashion our opinions accordingly?

I remember a relevant anecdote told by the late Governor Adlai E. Stevenson at Harvard's Godkin Lectures in 1954. It concerned a French revolutionary who was awakened from sleep by a disturbance outside his window. He ran to his window in great agitation, muttering, "The mob is in the street. I must see which way they are going, for I am their leader."

Surely a party worth its name does not junk its heritage and principles simply because the majority disagrees with it. On the contrary, it works all the harder to convince the majority. "My concern is not whether God is on our side," said President Lincoln during the dark days of the Civil War, "but whether we are on God's side."

I know of no satisfactory solution to this dilemma. Political parties are expected to lead the nation on the basis of their principles; yet they are also expected to court the public and win elections. They are expected to mold public opinion, but also to reflect it. A party that sweeps to victory by sacrificing all principles is no better than another which suffers steady defeats by refusing to disentangle itself from any principles, however outmoded. Every party must strike a balance somewhere between satisfying the mood of the majority and the dictates of the party's conscience, between being popular and being courageous, between leading and being led.

But I do not feel we are now on the horns of this dilemma. I believe our approach to national issues has been not only unpopular, but wrong. I think we are being rejected by the majority not because *they* are unable to understand the "true" American values we represent, but because *we* have been unable to understand many of their problems and aspirations.

I cannot hope that all Republicans will agree with me, for attachment to principle is profoundly important in American politics. I realize that to many it is unconvincing to offer our electoral losses as proof positive of our failures. "I'd rather be right than President" is an honored American tradition.

Perhaps the conflict between a party's need to win elections and its obligation to defend what it considers right can be resolved only by resorting to common sense. Surely there is *some* correlation between America's voting habits and the validity of our principles. Surely steady repudiation at the polls ought to suggest at least that we are failing not only in terms of popularity but also in terms of principle. Surely the way the political winds are blowing — when they blow with the persistence of tradewinds

[125]

— has *something* to do with how a party formulates its positions. Surely the willingness to disdain popular opinion ("I don't care if we *ever* win an election again, I'm going to stand on my principles") is going too far. But many Republican leaders do not seem to care whether we win a national election. "Let the party lose elections" — they say or imply — "as long as we are right." But losing elections defeats the very purpose of a political party. The Republican Party has been represented by many leaders who seem to believe in the "rule or ruin" theory, which is disastrous for an American political party.

"Political parties exist to win elections, not celebrate a sentiment," Roland N. Stromberg has written in *Republicanism Reappraised*. Perhaps that statement is too neat, too simple. But common sense suggests that *we* may be wrong, not the majority. Common sense suggests that a party can accomplish few of its objectives without winning elections. And common sense also suggests that the very nature of the democratic process is designed to give a hearing to all principles, but also to designate those which are more consistently favored by more voters as "right."

I do not want to be guilty of oversimplification. But this does seem to me basically a simple issue even though many Republican politicians and political scientists have made it sound complex. It is futile to proclaim our principles as Republicans while Democrats control the destiny of the nation. We must win elections in order to accomplish our goals. These are the simple political truths.

It is not always possible to link electoral failure with a failure of principle, but in our case, after thirty-five years, I believe some basis for the connection exists.

My point is that the Democrats have not won during these past thirty-five years so much as we have lost. As so often happens in military campaigns, it has not been Democratic brilliance in the field which accounted for the victories, so much as Republican hesitancy and retreats, which have often approached the appearance of unwillingness to fight. Had the Democrats been strong, united and efficient, possessed of solid principles and practical techniques for political warfare, there would be little to regret — we could have won honor in defeat. But the Democrats of 1930–1965 hardly fit that description. The painful truth is that we are being defeated by Democratic blunderers. We have not fought our best fight.

TWELVE

✤ ✤ ✤

The First Step Forward

I HAVE been describing some shortcomings of Republican leadership, shortcomings that many writers have found easy to locate and document. But it is always more difficult to suggest practical, workable alternatives. Granted the labors of full recovery will be difficult and protracted — how ought we to proceed? We are eager to pull on our boots and start the long march toward majority status — but in which direction ought we to go? Is it realistic to hope for recovery by our own efforts, or are we fated to wait passively until new historical forces in a new generation may (or may not!) offer us another opportunity to govern?

But this is a rhetorical question. No practicing politician should wait passively for historical forces to push his party into office. Let me, therefore, suggest a course of action which I believe will carry the Republican Party to rehabilitation and eventual triumph.

I think we must first rid ourselves of that which has weakened the competitive powers of the party. This has always been the task of defeated parties: to jettison old ideas and formulas that have lost their appeal; to cast off that which, however well it may have worked in the past, cannot compete in the politics of the present or future. There are many historical precedents here and abroad that demonstrate how politicians working to revitalize their defeated parties "got rid of what had to go," as a political historian has put it, "as realists, putting aside the childish luxury of attachment to past glories." Quite obviously, the Republican Party must leave something behind before it can go forward.

Let us examine a historical parallel. In the post–Civil War period, the Democratic Party faced a plight more dismal than our present one. In terms of popularity and prospects, they were worse off than we are today. For decades, they had been defeated, disorganized and discredited. They offered the country no attractive alternative programs. They stood for weak government and states' rights, laissez-faire and agrarianism — just at the time when America was entering the industrial age, which made all these approaches in their traditional forms irrelevant and obsolete. The heritage of Thomas Jefferson, the party's founder, hobbled the Democrats. Jefferson had a morbid distrust of industry, the city, and especially the urban working class. "The mobs of great cities," Jefferson wrote, "add just so much to the support of pure government, as sores do to the strength of the human body."

In short, the Democrats were crippled by a profoundly unfavorable image and by a set of principles which could only *keep* their image unfavorable. How then did they reverse their fortunes in this century? Their leaders were realists. They discarded their old dogmas of sectionalism, weak government and their mystical attachment to the virtue of small farms. They maintained the best of their philosophical heritage — Jefferson's concern with the "common" man — but adapted it to new circumstances. Where Jefferson's romantic notions proved illusory in an industrial age, the Democrats quietly put them aside to seek useful substitutes — precisely in the cities and factories which Jefferson abhorred. When at last they realized there was no hope of resurrecting their dead doctrines, the Democrats buried them. And we must bury ours.

What must we discard before we can go forward? The answer suggests itself from the causes of the party's decline. I believe the mood of negativism, of retrenchment, of avoiding the real issues by talking in slogans — and above all, our overriding, overwhelming distrust of "big government" as the Great Evil of our time — must be abandoned. And the central error of contemporary Republicanism is this tendency to regard "massive" federal government as an adversary. Of course there are inconveniences, annoyances, even dangers inherent in the existence and operation of a strong central government. But it is a great mistake to believe and to propagate the idea that government, even central government, is the natural adversary of the American people. Our real adversaries are not the programs and operations of government, but the "massive" conditions of twentieth-century American life which gave birth to "massive" government. Our real adversaries are the circumstances that lead to the cluttering of our land and our airwaves, the deterioration of our cities and countryside; the threat of total war, hot and cold; the accumulation of racial resentments and pent-up aspirations and, above all, a land shrinking in distances and exploding in population. Let us not, as the conservative poet Samuel Taylor Coleridge warned, make "the error of attributing to governments a talismanic influence over our virtues and our happiness, as if governments were not rather effects than causes."

It has been argued that rights are not guarantees by the government but guarantees against the government. This kind of approach to government can lead only to sterile passivity. For I think it is obvious that most rights are meaningless without guarantees and participation by government. This is true of the traditional American rights: the right to a fair trial, to participate in elections, to an elementary education. What could these rights mean without implementation by government? And it is even more true of the newer rights presupposed in our expanded concept of democracy — the right to a decent minimum wage, to an education commensurate with one's natural abilities, and to medical care for the aged.

How easy it is to pretend that big government is the source of our social problems — as if nothing else big had happened in the twentieth century; as if the problems of a complex technical society would somehow disappear if only we would "reverse the trend toward centralized government." What about all the other trends in our life — will they reverse themselves or regulate themselves so as to produce the greatest good for the greatest number? Does anyone seriously believe that order, education, beauty, opportunity, racial justice and social betterment are going to produce themselves without participation by government?

Science, technology, industry, economic necessity, intellectual thought are responsible for establishing the essential conditions and tone of America — not government.

We live and work where we do, enjoy the comforts and suffer the frustrations we do, entertain the dissatisfactions and aspirations we do, not by the order of government, but by the dictates of America's underlying social and economic forces. And if we are dissatisfied with aspects of our environment — our slums, polluted air, inadequate education and transportation, tense racial conflicts — we ought to remember that government is not the cause of these conditions but an agency that can be used to correct them. The effect of the automobile upon American life, for example, is incalculably greater than government's efforts to deal with some of the problems created by the automobile. Obviously, government does not cause deaths on the nation's highways, pollution of the nation's air by exhaust fumes, and suffocation of the nation's cities by hopeless traffic — but who would deny government's obligation to ameliorate these conditions?

I am suggesting that a self-confident political party seeking the opportunity to govern does not spend its time campaigning against government. This is no longer effective. "In general," it was reported by Philip Converse et al. in 1965 in the *American Political Science Review,* "the mass of public opinion has been quite unsympathetic to traditional Republican thinking in areas of social welfare and other domestic problems for several decades. A major Goldwater theme involved attacks against the increasingly heavy hand of 'big government,' yet this struck little in the way of a responsive chord. Most Americans in the more numerous occupational strata do not appear to feel governmental presence in any oppressive day-to-day manner. Among those more aware of the practices and potentials of federal government, a slight majority feels that if anything, governmental services and protections are inadequate rather than overdone."

Few voters fully believe in the sincerity of Republican campaigns against government. For when we *are* in office, we use the powers of government as all governing parties must — constructively and positively, to attack the problems of our society.

"In the years of governing the United States," Theodore White wrote in 1965, "the Republicans have, of course, immeasurably added to the reach of government authority, and more than honorably acquitted themselves of the great tasks thrust upon them. From the establishment of the Department of Agriculture in 1812 to Eisenhower's Federal Highway Act of 1956, the record of Republican achievement is one of massive acceptance of government responsibility. But the Republicans do not campaign on such issues. They campaign, generally, against government."

Let us begin to talk and act as we would if we were the governing party instead of the perpetual opposition. Let us attack the abuses and problems that damage the quality of American life, not the Democratic attempts, effectual or ineffectual, to cope with them. And let us attack these problems with knowledge and intelligence in the spirit of Theodore Roosevelt: "I'm interested in the next step," he said, "not the two hundredth." Let us take the next step. Let us devise proposals of our own — answers, not arguments. Let us face the problems confronting America.

THIRTEEN

✤ ✤ ✤

Startling Contrasts in American Life

WHAT are the domestic problems confronting America which the Republican Party must face? In a
sense, some of them are created by affluence and luxury —
by the forces which have made us incomparably richer
than any other people, yet always ambitious for improvement. Pioneering inevitably means problems and, in many
ways, America is still the world's pioneer among democratic
nations. Many of our problems, therefore, can be welcomed
as potential instruments of further progress. And if our
problems sometimes appear more agonizing than those of
other countries, that is often because our idealism is
stronger, our goals higher, our demands upon ourselves
and upon our government more stringent, and despite certain glaring lapses, our progress toward a reasonably
comfortable, secure and meaningful life for all our citizens
is greater than elsewhere.

America is not in a grave state of domestic crisis — or
more accurately, more grave than what we ordinarily face.
Books by politicians require a sense of drama; many of us
therefore tend to exaggerate the urgency of present or
impending emergencies. But each generation has its

"emergencies." Were I a historian or political scientist, I should like to develop a hypothesis of permanent emergency or permanent crisis. None that we face now is more difficult than others we have weathered before. None is in any way severe enough to justify a drastically new approach to the traditional American relationship of government to the governed. None requires any alteration in the essentially private nature of our society and economy.

This having been said, however, let me mention some of the problems themselves. For they *are* severe enough to justify our concentrated attention, and many of them can be attacked through a traditionally American — and Republican — approach to government: by helping the less privileged members of society to help themselves.

If there is a central theme running through those of America's contemporary problems that are the legitimate interest of government, it might be described as the startling unevenness in the quality of our national life. I shall not argue whether that quality is outrageously low compared to other Western nations — as our detractors suggest — or supremely high, as many superpatriots insist. The point is simply that many aspects of our national life beg for improvement. Poverty blights the surface of America, in major areas of our material, spiritual, educational and esthetic environment. We cannot measure our success as a society by comparing ourselves to poorer nations. The only fair comparison measures our own achievements against our own potentialities and capabilities. And who can claim that we are remotely close to fulfilling our potential for sustained excellence in our daily lives?

By "startling unevenness in the quality of our national

life" I mean the very sharp contrasts that exist, often side by side, in the lives of almost all of us. Take a half-hour walk through any of our major cities, and if you look at the sights as if for the first time instead of accepting them as "natural," you will, I think, be astonished at the often staggering and inexplicable juxtaposition of wealth and poverty, beauty and ugliness, progress and stagnation, achievement and failure. Many of the homes are lavish beyond comparison, yet the facilities for public relaxation in our cities can only be called primitive. We have incredible appliances for cleaning our offices — and inexcusably dirty streets. Private cars are magnificently shaped and equipped, but public transportation systems seem to be operated to test passengers' capacity to endure discomfort. Immense sums are spent to air-condition homes, offices and public buildings, but insignificant amounts are allocated to eliminate the dangerous pollution in our atmosphere. Stores are stocked with a dazzling assortment of goods and products, but schools are understaffed and underequipped. Comforts of all sorts are enjoyed by the majority of Americans, but despair, anger, crime, as well as physical decay, are growing in our spreading slums. Ever taller skyscrapers reach upward splendidly, while ever more inadequate parks shrink in comparison to the need for them. Ever more efficient business organizations contrast strikingly with ever more strained public services. Billions of dollars are spent for neon signs advertising every conceivable product — but we "cannot afford" to plant trees and flowers in downtown business sections. The city-dweller can purchase almost all of the world's most desirable goods, but he cannot purchase security as he strolls through the park after dark. In short, many

Americans are being deprived of beauty, comfort, security and a sense of well-being because we are failing to solve problems which are in our power to solve.

Take a ride to the country and you will see similarly startling contrasts. Enormously expensive and efficient highways are flanked by billboards, junk yards, and other forms of cancerous blight. More and more of the roads leading from our cities are being transformed into breeding grounds for suburban slums. More and more of the country's unparalleled natural beauty is being ravished by thoughtless exploitation. The number of pleasure boats has multiplied astronomically, but clean water in which to enjoy boating, fishing and bathing is rapidly disappearing. More and more people have the means to enjoy more and longer vacations, but unspoiled countryside and beaches are less and less available to most Americans. We have developed superb ingenuity for solving technological problems and creating technical marvels; yet because of a curious lack of proportion, we produce and tolerate vast areas of tawdriness and ugliness which debase our culture. We seem to be giving to ourselves with one hand and taking away with the other. We have not lacked the resources or skill to correct this imbalance. We have lacked the determination and the leadership to do it.

In certain areas, American society has been phenomenally successful. Yet our successes are undermined by structural flaws. We have enormous wealth, yet few of us are satisfied with how our wealth is used. More and more, we are concerned with the quality of our lives measured in terms of that beauty, balance and nobility which truly distinguish a civilization. And although our standard of living is miraculous, our standards of taste and our concern for beauty and order in our daily lives are disappointing. "As a people," wrote August Heckscher in the report issued by President Eisenhower's Commission on National Goals, "we face the question today whether our cultural standards can indeed be brought into balance with our material well-being."

But there is something even more disappointing in American life than the uneven development of our physical resources. Our misuse of human resources is far worse. We are the most productive and prosperous nation on earth — yet we tolerate mass ignorance, poverty and unemployment among our people. Some forty million of our people have not been able to "cash in" on the American Dream. In the midst of our plenty and progress, we have despair, disillusionment and defeatism among people who are shackled by generations of acquired disadvantages. It is in terms of human lives that the contrasts in American life are most startling.

These contrasts will not destroy America, but they will keep her from attaining her potential greatness. They affect some of us more than others, but in the long run, they hurt us all, even the richest and most protected Americans. For none of us can fully escape from their ill effects. The quality of American life is the sum total of the quality of its various parts. Even upper-middle-class suburbanites who think they have escaped are paying dearly. "You can run," as Joe Louis has said in a different context, "but you can't hide."

These are the problems with which the Republican Party must grapple. Republican leaders often talk about America the land of opportunity, and about the inherent worth and dignity of every individual American. And if we are serious about these statements, and I think we are, we face a vast amount of rethinking and planning. Beyond question, something monumental must be done. It is hypocritical to continue to talk of equality of opportunity and the blessings of individual enterprise when millions of individual Americans are unable to compete. Until beauty, justice and greatness are available to all Americans, the American Dream will never be realized.

It is morally right that we concern ourselves with these problems and that is enough reason for our concern. But what is morally right, or rather what becomes morally important at a given moment in political history often becomes sound politics as well. Sheer political advantage also requires that we find solutions to these problems. America's greatness, progress and destiny of which we talk will be decided largely in terms of how these problems are resolved. They are now rising to the surface of national consciousness as did the problems of the New Deal in another era. We must propose solutions. The Democrats will. And however imperfect their solutions, they will reap electoral advantages from them as they have for the past thirty-five years if we fail to seize our opportunity. But as important as specific solutions are, a framework for thinking about them is even more important. More than anything, the Republican Party has lacked a viable framework which is consistent with its traditions and yet relevant to the needs of the times. I shall discuss three of America's most pressing problems, therefore, and suggest a Republican approach to them.

✥ ✥ ✥

The Problem of Poverty

POVERTY, in its broadest sense, describes what is most undesirable in American life. It has been a plague on mankind since the beginning of history. Most of the world's people have been abysmally poor — too poor to secure enough food for themselves and their families. And most of the world's people are still abysmally poor. Why, then, has *American* poverty become a critical political issue?

I think it has become a critical political issue for the reason that always makes issues politically critical: the time for its solution has arrived. The economic means to eliminate poverty are at our disposal. Awareness of the problem has become widespread. All the tangible and intangible factors which together shape the national consciousness indicate that the elimination of poverty amidst staggering plenty — indeed, amidst surplus — must be the next step in the ceaseless process of democratization. Poverty can no longer be ignored.

America's poor have become more and more segregated from the rest of the nation. Poverty has always been off the beaten path, and as the rich two-thirds of Americans grow richer — grow more concerned with automobiles, television sets, summer and winter vacations, homes in the suburbs — the poor are less and less apt to be known to them. The paths of the "two Americas" rarely cross. But the writings of social scientists, journalists and politicians in the past three or four years have brought American poverty to the attention of millions of middle- and upper-class Americans. American poverty is now the subject of magazine and newspaper articles as well as television documentaries. And the few statistics I shall cite are becoming common knowledge.

Of the forty-seven million American families in 1963, over a fifth had total family incomes of less than three thousand dollars a year — less than sixty dollars a week. In 1963 from a fifth to a third of our people were living in, or on the borderline of, poverty. Five and a half million American families — containing over seventeen million people, almost half of them children — survive on incomes of less than two thousand dollars a year — less than forty dollars a week. Of America's "single-person" families, five million — roughly forty-five per cent — have total incomes of less than fifteen hundred dollars a year, and thirty per cent exist on less than one thousand dollars a year — less than twenty dollars a week! Of all American statistics, these are the most disturbing.

Poverty in America does not mean starvation. It does not mean utter destitution, hunger or homelessness as it does for hundreds of millions of the poor of Asia, Africa and Latin America. But it does mean substandard medical care, substandard education and substandard cultural influences, all of which doom the children of the poor to remain poor unless blessed by extraordinary ability or great good fortune. It means a shorter life plagued by more frequent physical and mental disease; a smaller body and a less developed mind. It means a set of values dictated not by the ambition of the American Dream, but by the rules of survival on relief, unemployment checks and subsistent wages. And it means passing aimless days on street corners and the porches of rural shacks. It means stagnation.

Roughly forty to fifty million Americans are living in a twentieth-century subculture — the victims, rather than the beneficiaries, of our meteoric advance in knowledge, technology, standards of education and comfort. These forty to fifty million people are the rejects of our otherwise magnificently affluent society — a people who never had the skills to "climb aboard," or who were never allowed to climb aboard, while American society raced forward. Or they are people whose skills were rendered obsolete by the advance. In all these cases, the people involved find it increasingly difficult to catch up. They are the dishwashers, the harvest workers, the sharecroppers, the odd-jobs men, the former coal miners, the elevator operators, the displaced conveyor-line operators, the "errand boys," the nonunionized store clerks, the skilled workers displaced by automation — and always, the masses of untrained, unequipped, and incompetent who lack that minimum of economic value to break into the vibrant world of business and organized labor, and who must exist, hand to mouth, on woefully inadequate wages or one form or another of doles.

One-third of the forty million to fifty million poor Americans are children under eighteen. A conservative estimate places the number of children condemned to almost certain poverty, and to rear *their* children in even greater relative poverty, at twelve million! They will live lives of sickness, starchy foods, aimlessness, and probably crime. They will know almost nothing of human dignity because almost nothing they are capable of performing is dignified according to the values of our society. On the average, they will work only six months a year and earn, on the average, less than half a skilled factory worker's hourly pay. Something is drastically wrong when any American child is born with such great odds against living a moderately successful and happy life.

There are exceptions, of course, which are widely publicized for the purpose of suggesting that the slum need not stunt a young person's growth, but on the contrary, should stimulate it. But these are indeed exceptions, and they are very rare. When shining examples are cited — as they sometimes are — as proof that the poor can rise from the slums, I remember the reaction of Senator Robert F. Wagner of New York when he was used as such an example. "That is the most God-awful bunk," Senator Wagner replied. "I came through it, yes. That was luck, luck, luck. Think of the others."

Social scientists disagree about the statistics of poverty. Some say there are thirty-five million "poor" Americans; others put the figure at fifty million. Some feel a family income of three thousand dollars a year constitutes poverty; others put that figure at twenty-five hundred dollars. Some place widows whose sole source of support is a monthly social security check for sixty-five dollars —

roughly, the median social security benefit for widows —
in the category of the poor; others place them in a different category. Some say America's poor number a fifth of
our population; others place the figure at a third.

One can debate the accuracy and interpretation of
these figures, and one can argue about the precise point
at which a person or a family can be said to be living in
poverty. But such arguments are irrelevant. The essential
fact is that for a large number of our people, life is a grim,
degrading ordeal of bad food, bad health, ignorance and
wretchedness. And this in a nation rich beyond belief!

Poverty is not a collection of statistics. It is fathers who
cannot feed their children, and children who are compelled literally to steal food. It is families living in bitterness and rejection; pupils eager to go to school (if only to
get their single nourishing meal of the day) but pre-
vented by lack of shoes; teenagers with no plans, no promise, and little hope for a productive life. It is a marginal
existence on the fringes of society, a kind of half-life
lived in a culture which is almost totally unlike that of "normal" America. "Abandon all hope, ye who enter here" is
the motto fixed on the gate of hell in Dante's *Inferno*. It
applies as well to millions of Americans born into poverty.

We can derive no comfort from the knowledge that
America's poor are in fact vastly richer than the poor of
Asia, Africa, Latin America and Russia. For poverty must
be judged relative to average standards in one's own country, not the poor of distant lands. In a sense, America's
poor are worse off than the poor of, say, India. For, unfortunately, poverty is the rule in India, not the exception.
A poor Indian is not isolated from the normal conditions

of his national life. A poor American, however, is an alien, very nearly an untouchable. He has almost no contact with anything dynamic in America. The English states- man William Pitt said that "poverty is no disgrace but it is damned annoying." But as Professor John Kenneth Gal- braith, the noted economist, has countered, poverty in contemporary America is "not annoying but it is a dis- grace."

America's poor are not only isolated from the rest of the nation; they are also "immunized from progress." Tens of millions of immigrants who flocked to America from east- ern, central and southern Europe in the nineteenth cen- tury were poor too, and in many cases, exploited. But they were not nearly so helpless as America's contemporary poor. The opportunities for the poor were then far greater: the route from unskilled laborer, warehouse helper, even shoeshine boy to success was a well-marked one, and if it required hard work and endurance, it was not strewn with insurmountable obstacles. The immi- grants had the skills for success, or could acquire them with reasonable effort. For what was then most needed were strong hands and strong backs. And most important, ambition, that crucial prerequisite for success that most immigrants had in abundance.

Today's poor, however, see no clearly marked paths, but only obstacles. They are "technological illiterates" in an age when technology — education and particularly spe- cialized education — is the *sine qua non* of success. They have no employable skills and little understanding of how to acquire them. They know that unskilled labor leads to nothing but eventual unemployment, and therefore they are filled with apathy and despair. They are a beaten people because they lack a sense of where to begin. "Poverty," Professor Galbraith has observed, "is self-perpetuating because the poorest communities are poorest in the services which would eliminate it." Hopelessness is bequeathed from father to son, gaining in intensity with each generation because the skills needed to break free of it are greater with each generation.

Until recently, it was assumed that as the productivity and wealth of America increased, poverty would shrink and eventually disappear. But that has not happened. The poverty of Americans in the "mainstream" of society *has* disappeared, but the poverty of the outcasts has solidified into semi-permanence. Not only have those outside the mainstream become relatively poorer compared to the rest of the nation; more important, the chances for the poor to enter the mainstream have become fewer. The gap between those who have employable skills or suitable education and those who are unskilled, uneducated, unemployed — and unemployable — grows greater in direct proportion to the economic and cultural development of American society. The barriers that prevent immigration from poor to rich America are ever more difficult to scale. The poor become poorer in a thousand ways — the most tragic of them in the opportunity, and therefore the ambition, to "make it."

This is one of the gravest problems of contemporary America — a problem which, if unsolved, will establish a permanently underprivileged and hostile class of a fourth of all Americans, shattering the American Dream of the just and classless society.

An "all out" offensive against poverty is going to take place whether the Republican Party directs it or not. Morally and politically, this is a challenge that the Republican Party can no longer ignore.

FIFTEEN

The Problem of Civil Rights

THE nation's most urgent and dramatic domestic problem concerns equality for its more than twenty million
nonwhites. No achievement, however spectacular, in other
areas of our national life can obscure the magnitude of
this problem. The conquest of space, the soaring increase
in our national wealth, the flowering of our arts and sciences — our finest achievements are tarnished while more
than a tenth of all Americans remain second-class citizens
because of the color of their skins. America's future as the
champion of world democracy depends largely on how —
and how quickly — racial inequality is eliminated.

National ideals and personal consciences dictate that
Americans commit themselves to this goal with total re-
solve. America's respect among other peoples of the world
is at stake. For America is being judged by a world increasingly concerned about the reality rather than the
rhetoric of democracy. And America is being judged by a
world increasingly conscious about the color of skin.

But this is common knowledge. Almost all Americans
now sense the urgency of the problem — if not its depth.
The litany of wretched facts and figures testifying to the

effects of discrimination is becoming well known. News of racial tension and conflict, and frantic attempts to ease them, monopolize our front pages. Racial oppression is another of the great social issues on which political parties rise or fall. It is produced by a thousand tangible and intangible historical forces reacting in concert. Nothing can dispel these forces. The time for the resolution of the issue has arrived.

Progress toward racial equality in the United States had been slow until the post–World War II era. I remember well the discouragement of World War II. I was assigned to the 366th Combat Infantry Regiment, an all-Negro unit of Mark Clark's Fifth Army, fighting in the Apennine Mountains of Italy. We were fighting hard and fighting well. Our morale was high in spite of heavy casualties. And yet there was an undercurrent of resentment in the regiment. For the regiment was segregated. In a hundred subtle and not-so-subtle ways, we were treated as second-class soldiers. Our soldiers (first-class by any definition) asked, "Why are *we* fighting this war? It's supposed to be a war against Nazism — against racism and for democracy. Well, what about *us?* Why are black men fighting a white man's war? What's all this double-talk about democracy?" They were not easy questions to answer. I tried to explain that the first task was to defeat the common enemy. And I asked them to bear with America's racial injustices until the war was won. But I knew that this was no more than a rationalization.

In the twenty years since World War II, America has taken great strides toward eliminating some forms of racial injustice. This could not have been achieved without a remarkable moral awakening by great numbers of white Americans. But more than anyone else, Negro Americans — especially those in the civil rights movement — are responsible for those great strides.

Nothing I might say about the civil rights movement would give it the recognition and praise it deserves. It is a magnificent crusade that expresses the very essence of American — and human — ideals. The courage, endurance, common sense and tactical genius of its leaders, such as A. Philip Randolph and Martin Luther King, are superb. Wedding restraint with action, they have achieved remarkable success against seemingly impossible odds.

How have the civil rights leaders managed to keep the movement nonviolent despite the violence endured by civil rights workers? They have been accused of radicalism, but their only radical action has been exposing the radicalism of others. They have developed superb techniques of protest, grounded in high legal and moral principles. They have moved millions of Negroes — and millions more whites — to feel a sense of personal involvement. The sit-ins and demonstrations, marches and boycotts, lawsuits and voter registration drives — these programs have been brilliantly executed. And who can claim that without these vast labors a hundredth of the progress of the last decade would have been achieved? The debt of Americans to the men and women, black and white, who are active in the struggle is incalculable. Here is a peaceful crusade that is going to remake America in the image of her constitutional principles at last, and when the history of this century is written, the movement may well be singled out as its most important social transformation.

The American Negro must win allies, not conquer adversaries. For the harsh reality is that we are engaged in a struggle for equality, and we are a small minority. We are not only a minority in terms of population. The disproportion in our material resources is far more overwhelming. There are few Negroes of great wealth. Negro votes have become significant in pivotal elections, but relative to the white vote, they are still a small percentage. Ownership of industry and the means of communication; control of local, state and federal government; membership in what is called the "power elite" — these are securely in the possession of white Americans. Even if there were a revolutionary tradition in America, Negroes would be foolhardy to resort to revolution. A hot war against whites would be, on strategic grounds alone, pure madness. And Negro leaders and civil rights organizations have never advocated violence. In Watts and in the few other places where violence has flared, it has not been caused by the civil rights movement but by the eruption of the social and economic volcano which smolders in the ghettos and slums of America. The Negro realizes that for victory we need allies. And we need all of the moral, legal, economic and political assistance that allies can offer. To those who oppose us, our strategy must be based on influence and inducement, on altering thought patterns and old standards — on appeal to hearts and minds. For the best way to defeat an enemy is to make of him a friend. Not the sword, but persuasion. And this fortunately has been recognized by those civil rights leaders who are genuinely dedicated to the cause of civil rights.

In some aspects, progress toward racial justice in America has been spectacular. And yet, in other, more important aspects, we have only begun — and not seriously begun

— to inch ahead. America is confused about whether to rejoice at what has been accomplished or to despair at what yet needs to be done. For we have only scratched the surface and revealed the enormity of the task ahead.

The Civil Rights Act of 1964 and the Voting Rights Act of 1965 were enacted amidst great enthusiasm and optimism as a political response to the protest and electoral power of Negroes and our allies. They have been called an "end to a beginning." But in their daily lives, the great masses of Negro Americans remain untouched by this legislation. For alone, the Civil Rights and Voting Rights Acts cannot accomplish what must be accomplished in the future: giving America's nonwhites the same start in life as other Americans. Certainly they are splendid pieces of legislation, by far the most valuable in the history of America's advance toward equal rights. Yet they are symbols of the fundamental inadequacy of this approach to the problems of racial inequality. For underneath the Negro concern for equal rights lies the source of his real problems: unequal jobs, education, skills, cultural development and a frustrated ambition for success.

Freedom in the sense of the right to be hired for any job, to attend any school, live in any apartment, eat in any restaurant — even freedom to vote — though essential, cannot solve the real problems. Even with all the freedom in the world, the great majority of Negroes would be woefully ill-equipped to make a reasonably equal life for themselves in America's competitive society. Centuries of oppression have given them staggering handicaps. It is to this cruel fact that the nation's attention must be devoted. And it is to this cruel fact that the Republican Party must devote its attention.

The Problem of Civil Rights

An opportunity is, of course, a good beginning — but relatively meaningless so long as the people involved are unable to make use of that opportunity. While America has made heartening progress in providing some opportunities for Negroes, the ability of Negroes to make use of them has been actually declining! A few statistics will illustrate this discouraging condition. The rate of Negro unemployment is more than double that of whites. Most Americans are now aware of the sharp disparity between the income of Negroes and whites. In 1962 the average white family income was $5642, while $3023 was the average Negro family income. Forty per cent of the Negroes employed worked in the lowest-paying jobs, as farm laborers and unskilled workers.

Even in jobs requiring identical skills, the contrast in income is astonishing. The average Negro truck driver and delivery man earns $2600 a year, while the average white truck driver and delivery man earns $4500. Up and down the employment scale, in every category, similar conditions prevail. A Negro college graduate's life income is, on the average, only slightly more than half of a white college graduate's life income. The average *college*-educated Negro earns even less during his lifetime than the average white *high school* graduate. In short, the average Negro earns roughly half the wages earned by the average white. And this half is simply too little to provide for the investment in education, training and cultural development to earn more.

This widening gap in these most fundamental criteria of equality has caused widespread protest and justifiable bitterness among Negroes. But bitterness, however justified, will not solve Negro problems. And bitterness, like preju-

[153]

dice, does more harm to those who harbor it than to those against whom it is directed. Protest, on the other hand, has been a valuable weapon in the struggle for equality. For with all of its racial injustice, America is built around a core of moral principles, and once national attention is focused on an injustice, the great majority of Americans react in terms of those principles.

The good people of America, the typical Americans, those who live in the South as well as in the rest of the country, are predisposed, now, to right the wrongs of racial injustice. They are now opposed to discrimination in theory. But they are concerned, in their daily lives, with a great deal more than theory. "Look," a fourth-generation American is likely to say, "I've denied the Negroes nothing. Perhaps my great-grandfather did, and maybe my grandfather. But not me. I'm horrified at the thought of slavery and I'm against discrimination. But if you want to get ahead, you've got to work for it just like everyone else does; you have no claim against me." A first-generation American is likely to say: "I was born in Brooklyn, and I never had a thing to do with exploiting Negroes. What do I owe the Negro? My father came to America because he couldn't make out in the old country. He finally got a little piece of land (or little store or lowly job) and he gave his whole life to it. I've worked all my life too, and I'm not going to give up anything, because I never mistreated anyone, black or white. I've built myself a decent life, and brother, if you want one, you've got to get it for yourself." The fact is that, fortunately for them, none of these Americans was confronted with the problems with which the American Negro has suffered and in the main is still suffering. But the fact is also that the thoughts of these Americans are widely shared and are the thoughts with which the nation and the Negro must be concerned.

The American Negro does not expect American whites to pay personal damages for the evils of an entire system. They know that white Americans have their own problems in securing good schools, neighbors, jobs — in securing the good life for themselves and their own children. They realize that however contrite some Americans may feel over the oppression of Negroes, America remains a highly competitive society, and in the final analysis Negroes will stand or fall in the competition on the basis of their ambitions, skills and achievements. What the Negro expects, wants and now demands is the removal of all barriers which deny him the opportunity to improve his lot and to compete on equal ground with his fellow Americans.

The Negro wants to live in an integrated society with all that that implies. He no longer is willing to live on the outside looking in. He wants his children to attend good schools. But he also wants them to attend integrated schools. He wants school bussing as necessary but temporary relief in the establishment of integrated schools. But he also wants the destruction of the Negro ghetto which, among other benefits, will establish permanent school integration. He wants equal job opportunities and equal pay for equal skills and equal services. For he knows that with equal job opportunities he can improve his skills and services, which in turn will increase his income, thereby improving his standard of living.

When I speak of the disadvantaged Negro, I speak of the great majority of Negroes. I am aware that there is a small minority who have had the great fortune to share in the American Dream. I know of the relatively few Negroes who have attained considerable wealth primarily (and ironically) from the segregated system in which they have been forced to sell their goods and services. Progress has been made in the arts, religion, sports, politics, labor and business, to mention a few. But progress in terms of the masses of Negroes has barely begun. The small minority who have had the advantages to move out, move on, and move up still have problems common to all Negroes. In addition, they cannot close their eyes to the fact that the masses of Negroes, whence they have come, are still left far behind. The critical problems facing the masses of Negroes are the problems which advantaged Negroes and advantaged white Americans working together must help disadvantaged Negroes solve.

The "Negro" problem is not only a problem of ending segregation in eating places and schools, of insuring civil rights, or even of providing equal opportunities for each individual Negro to educate himself and his family, secure fruitful employment and create a meaningful life measured in the standards of contemporary America. All of these things are important; all of them still require a vast effort by civil rights groups, government, and especially by citizens and citizens' groups in every community. But these are only the first steps, dealing with surface symptoms of the problem. Legal equality can be meaningless when it masks a deep disparity in human ability.

It is in this most fundamental area of human ability where the real problems are spawned. Children of disadvantaged Negroes are born in a culturally deprived environment, and usually remain in it. Sociological studies have shown that by the time they reach kindergarten, black and white children born with equal intellectual ability have diverged markedly in their ability to profit from education. The cause is obvious: the cultural influences in disadvantaged Negro homes — vocabulary, books, exposure to music and ideas — are far poorer. All of the forces that determine personality have already exerted themselves to produce a disadvantaged child. The child cannot successfully compete in school, the adolescent in high school, the young adult in admission to college. And later as an adult, in competition for a good job. Family, neighborhood, friends, schools, vacations, reading matter, recreation — every aspect of the disadvantaged Negro child's surroundings helps to make him unequal. And even if the opportunities offered him at some point in his life are equal, he suffers grave disadvantages in competing for them. The gravest disadvantage lies in his motivation. He has simply not been inspired to study harder, work better, to improve his lot, because everything he has learned, consciously or instinctively, has taught him: What's the use? As Tolstoy said: "Man's greatest inhumanity to man has not been what he denied him, but what he has kept him from even wanting."

Lack of motivation and all the other disadvantages suffered by disadvantaged Negroes are rooted deep in their experience and consciousness. They are the products of generations of deprivation. While other minority groups were climbing the traditional ladder of success Negroes were being held back almost forceably by the color of their skins. And this, of course, had the expected results. Bitterness, rebelliousness, indifference, negativism and passiveness — these, together with cultural disadvantages, are passed from father to son, crippling each new generation's chances of overcoming them, even of dreaming of overcoming them. Equality of opportunity means little or nothing when, for those who need equality most, severe handicaps are built in.

In competitive America, skills, training, ambition, knowledge and acquaintances are what count — these are the products of investment and development over many generations. There is, I think, no other meaningful way to examine the "Negro" problem. And it is here that the Negro's needs are greatest. The ability to compete — man to man, skill for skill, degree for degree — will not be bestowed upon Negroes magically. Mere passage of time will solve nothing — indeed, the gap, as I have mentioned, is widening.

The solution will not be easy. It will require much more than passing and enforcing laws dealing with the surface aspects of equality of opportunity. It will require working with the human stuff which is the real measurement of equality. And yet the task, however massive, must be faced. Racial inequality permeates every aspect of our national life; no domestic or foreign issue is more important. Now that the pretense of "equal opportunity for all" has been exposed, the course of action we pursue to make the slogan real will determine the nature and content of American democracy for the remainder of this century.

The total elimination of racial inequality in America presents the Republican Party with a great challenge and a great opportunity. As Governor George Romney of Michigan has said, "the Republican Party has the opportunity to play the crucial role in rebuilding faith in the authentic American Revolution. . . . [It] must work without respite, [and] dedicate itself with unalloyed devotion to the task of securing equal rights for all Americans."

This is the issue, massive and complex, which the Republican Party must face; for the issue is pressing on the nation, and cries out for solution.

SIXTEEN

The Problem of Urban Centers

THE quality of American life is the quality of life lived in America's cities, for the great majority of Americans live in urban areas. By 1970 eighty per cent of our population will be living in these areas, most of them in a few dozen sprawling metropolitan centers. By 1980 some sixty million more Americans will be living in metropolitan areas than were living there in 1960. All of us are profoundly affected by the quality of city life, for the city is the center of things and even farmers spend part of their time in the center, shopping, sight-seeing, or taking advantage of the city's entertainments.

But most important, cities establish the tone of national life in this urban age. The tone of a twentieth-century civilization, of its art, commerce, and standards of excellence, is determined principally by what takes place in its nerve centers, the cities. Inevitably, commerce, industry, and intellectual activity are directed from there. Deterioration at the center cannot be compensated for by growth, however impressive, in the suburbs or anywhere else. What George Bernard Shaw said about English cities early in this century is even more pertinent to America today:

"Such poverty as we have today in all our great cities degrades the poor, and infects with its degradation the whole neighborhood in which they live. And whatever can degrade a neighborhood can degrade a city and a continent and finally the whole civilized world."

I emphasize deterioration because precisely that has been taking place in all of our great urban centers during the postwar decades. There have been pockets of progress and projects of renewal, but, on balance, the forces causing decay have been far more powerful. In most cities it has been very rapid decay, especially near the heart of the city. Even in New York City, which has the largest slum clearance program in the United States, the rate of deterioration is greater than the rate of construction of new housing. We are losing ground. We are confronted with another of the paradoxes of modern America: on the streets of the richest cities of the world's richest country, the quality of life measured in terms of beauty, security, comfort and a sense of civilized well-being has been declining markedly. Our brilliant ingenuity, our immense production, our fantastic wealth seem powerless to reverse the deterioration.

The problems of the cities are myriad, severe and complex. I have selected a few of the major ones in order to see whether they group themselves into patterns, and if so, whether the patterns lend themselves to a particular approach to problem-solving. The most visible problems are related to the spreading of ugliness and shrinkage of beauty. In some cases, even new buildings — monotonous glass-and-steel boxes, sacrificing architectural and esthetic considerations to commercial profit — compound the oppressiveness of our city centers. But the real breeding ground of ugliness is, of course, slums. A fifth or more of the people of the average American metropolitan center live in slums, with all that that implies in terms of overcrowding (large families living in a single room), filth (garbage in gutters and rats multiplying in tenements), and squalid streets. And many more city-dwellers, perhaps another fifth, live in cheerless, dreary areas fated to become slums. Nothing despoils America more than these cancerous urban eyesores.

And slums produce crime. Not all urban crime is spawned in the slums; a disturbing percentage of it is found in middle- and upper-class neighborhoods. But recent studies have shown that the slums are in fact what they have always been presumed to be: breeding grounds for crimes of violence.

We have recently witnessed an interesting debate on criminal statistics. The Federal Bureau of Investigation and police departments of several large cities have published evidence to indicate that the incidence of major crimes has risen by roughly ten per cent a year in the last decade. (This means that the crime rate has grown six times faster than the growth in population!) But other experts feel that the use of new statistical methods accounts for much of the increase. Whatever the merit of these arguments, the crime rate, particularly the rate of street crimes of violence involving mugging, molesting and murder, *is* rising startlingly. And the "fear rate" is rising even more rapidly.

Whole sections of our cities, including many of their loveliest parks, are considered unsafe by most people, certainly by night and increasingly by day. The risk of an unpleasant incident, if not an attack, grows greater year by year. One of America's chief sources of shame is the sense of insecurity pervading city streets, transportation systems and parks. "When I was a boy," the *New York Times* quoted a New Yorker in connection with the latest F.B.I. report on soaring crime statistics (a thirteen per cent nationwide increase in 1964), "we used to camp out in Central Park. Now you'd be crazy to go there at night." *Newsweek* quoted a middle-aged woman who lived alone in Manhattan. "I get home from work at six," she said. "The only thing that would make me go out before next morning is a fire."

Of all the increase in crime, the greatest part has been caused by youth, and this is all the more appalling. For in addition to the horrors one usually associates with juvenile crime, this statistic symbolizes the greatest shortcoming of our modern cities: failure to provide wholesome surroundings for our young people. Many city children lack the most elementary recreational facilities — space, air, playgrounds, ball parks; and in the larger cities thousands of teen-agers haunt the streets, unemployed, untrained, indifferent, and potentially lawless. Urban unemployment is highest among young people, especially those seeking their first jobs; their unemployment rate is roughly double that of adults. Ambition, hope and a sense of purpose is weakest where it ought to be strongest, among teen-agers and people in the early twenties.

And this leads us to another grave problem suffered by our major cities, the problem of public schools. Most city school systems are plagued by overcrowding, substandard teaching, and substandard facilities. Particularly in slum areas, teachers are more often than not compelled to spend most of the day maintaining a semblance of order and preventing violence; teaching in the traditional sense often seems utopian. Vocational training is especially weak and outmoded, and this aggravates yet another problem in the schools, the problem concerning "dropouts." The dropout rate is inordinately high, especially in low-income neighborhoods — and this has a much more sinister effect than it did a generation ago when the rate was also high. Before World War II, teenagers dropped out of school to go to work. Now they drop out with few chances and little hope of finding work. With the rapid decrease in unskilled and semiskilled jobs, most of them are joining the unemployed and unemployable, increasing the frustrations, tensions and crime rates of the cities.

Because the quality of many public schools has seriously deteriorated in the postwar decades, more and more middle-class parents are sending their children to private schools — which, in turn, helps accelerate the deterioration of the public schools. And this vicious cycle in the public school system reflects a much more serious vicious cycle in the city at large: more and more middle- and upper-class families are fleeing our cities altogether. In some of the larger cities, hundreds of thousands of families whose breadwinners are skilled and white collar workers, professional men and businessmen — traditionally the human backbone of cities — have joined the exodus to the suburbs to escape the problems I have been describing and others too numerous to describe. Quite simply, the city is no longer considered a desirable place in which to live by most middle- and upper-class families. The goal of most ambitious young couples is to leave the city as quickly as possible, so that they and their children can find security and comfort. In an age when the quality of a civilization depends largely upon the tone of life in its cities, this is a grim augury for America's future.

And as the middle and upper classes desert the city, dozens of problems are compounded by their absence. The city center changes character. Downtown business declines; hundreds of stores and shops, small and large, close permanently or move to the suburbs; tens of thousands of jobs are lost. Just at a time when the city's financial needs soar, its sources of revenue shrink. A prominent sociologist, Norton E. Long, has compared the central city to an aging automobile: it still retains some value, "but (like used cars) aging housing, stores and factories must accept lower returns, even in the face of rising maintenance costs." America's enormous mobility afforded by cars and trucks has made it cheaper for many businesses to leave the city entirely, instead of rebuilding or moving to another district. Long continues, "What is happening to the central city in the metropolitan area is indeed no more than what in the past has happened to neighborhoods within the central city itself. But whereas in the past the decay of one area in the city was compensated for by the growth of another, now the growth occurs almost exclusively outside the corporate limits of the central city and thus escapes sharing the burden of decay."

All major American cities are faced with this problem: a central city with declining property values, declining skills and prospects among its residents — with declining value in terms of everything that makes cities great — and at the same time greater and greater maintenance costs. The aging of the central cities' physical facilities and their settlement by unskilled, semiskilled, or unem-

[165]

ployed workers makes enormous demands on relief, welfare and other services, while producing minimal revenue. It also produces "jungle" schools and neighborhoods pervaded by an atmosphere of ugliness, bitterness and despair. These were the intensifying problems that led Henry W. Maier, the mayor of Milwaukee, to describe our metropolitan centers as "the dust bowls of the 1960's." Mayor Maier also pointed out that at a time when slum-dwellers outnumber farmers, our cities receive a mere one-thirteenth of federal funds allocated to farmers, and that more money is spent on a single space shot than on all federal assistance to urban renewal. Thus, the future of our cities is gravely menaced, and our response has been hopelessly inadequate.

Those who feel that alarmists exaggerate our urban problems point out that most American cities have been troubled by the same basic crises for over a century. Overcrowding, slums, crime, substandard education, unemployment and poverty — these have been the traditional problems of cities, and not only American cities. But the problems have intensified enormously during the last decade, so much so that their substance has changed together with their complexity. We seem to have crossed the boundary between hope and hopelessness: academicians, journalists, and even politicians are now speaking of our cities as "ungovernable."

The fate of grass roots democracy seems to be at stake, for, since most Americans live in cities, it is there that most Americans experience their only contact (or lack of contact) with local government. And city governments, overwhelmed by crises, are increasingly unable to demonstrate how local government can deal effectively with problems.

There *has* been a dramatic shift toward the worst in the last decade, and it is symbolized by the increasingly tense atmosphere surrounding racial conflicts, an atmosphere fraught with potential and actual violence. As the quality of American life improves markedly outside the city limits, the quality of life in the center grows relatively — and in some respects absolutely — worse. The paradox we have observed before pertains also to our cities. The rapid development of American technology and society seems not to guarantee progress in our city centers, but to make serious problems worse. There have always been slums in our cities — but now they are more angry and explosive. There has always been crime — but now it is more menacing to the security of the entire city. There have always been poor people — but now they seem more listless and hopeless, and seem to personify the decline of the city itself. There have always been frustrated minorities — but now, as *Newsweek* has deftly put it, "the melting pot no longer melts, it only boils."

Is there a pattern to these problems? I think there is. The same sets of self-perpetuating handicaps operate in our central cities as among our nonwhites and our poor. And there is a simple explanation for this phenomenon: the inner core of our cities is increasingly composed of precisely these nonwhites and poor. Until World War II, the American city was a rather broad-based collection, a cross section of American groups, with great economic, racial and sociological diversity. But in the last two decades, there has been an extraordinary rapid movement toward stratification and a one-class culture. The poor are squeezed into the inner core; around them are the middle class, separated by that invisible but increasingly insurmountable wall between those who have developed the human potential to succeed in American society and those who have not. Our major cities, in other words, are becoming giant ghettos. If statistics were needed to document this ominous social development, one could cite dozens. But again, this is a development observable to the naked eye.

The slum is not yet predominantly Negro, for whites living in urban poverty now outnumber Negroes. But this condition is changing too. If existing birthrate trends continue unchanged, seven of America's ten largest cities will have Negro majorities within a decade; in twenty years many more of our major cities will be populated predominantly by Negroes.

Not all the ills of our cities can be traced to the enormous increase in poor whites and nonwhites. There are also severe problems of traffic, air pollution, court backlogs, commuting and mass transportation, inadequate tax structures, and of obsolete governmental organization and procedure that are not directly related to the slum. But these technical problems are easily solved compared to the human problems of our cities. More and more, our urban centers house America's rejects — those who languish in the "backward" sectors of our culture — and any program for curing urban ills that does not concern itself with these fundamental causes is an exercise in self-delusion.

It would be pleasant to concern ourselves instead with the nation's successes, praising ourselves — justifiably — for the great works Americans have accomplished. But that will not help the nation. The vast increase (an increase of roughly one hundred and six million citizens) in American population that is expected between 1960 and

1985 will materialize almost entirely in metropolitan areas. Many of the new Americans will be poor, for the population growth among the urban poor is almost twice that of the national average. In New York City, for example, it is estimated that one-half of all new babies are being born to indigent parents. And many of them will be Negro. In 1960 one American in ten was nonwhite; in 1972 one adult in eight — and one child in five — will be nonwhite.

These are the urban problems that the nation and the Republican Party must face — momentous problems that no longer concern only minorities, but the very stuff of our national life. The Republican Party must not continue to turn its back on the city, or the city will continue to turn its back on us.

SEVENTEEN

The Democratic Party's Fundamental Flaw

I HAVE been arguing that for a generation we have been a perennial minority party with progressively shrinking support; that we have condemned ourselves to this position by clinging to obsolete theories when change is the law of life; that we must change our attitudes or remain an ineffective minority for the foreseeable future; and that the first change ought to be replacing antigovernment postures and slogans with a dispassionate, factual analysis of America's major problems — the real flaws in our national life. I have suggested that the country faces a battery of extremely serious problems generated by our chronic poor, our nonwhites, and our deteriorating city centers which are overflowing with poor whites and nonwhites.

These are the domestic problems that disturb the nation more than any others, and will disturb it more and more as popular awareness of their underlying causes grows. These are the major sources of tension and dissatisfaction in American life, and both will intensify unless the problems are resolved faster than the fast-growing discontent. These are now the major obstacles to that truly distinguished American Way of Life we all desire. It is the responsibility of the Republican Party to seek solutions for them. But what about our opposition — what about the Democrats? Haven't they pre-empted these problems as their own special domain? Aren't they considered by most voters to be the natural problem-solvers in these areas?

Many Republicans argue that our solutions will be judged in comparison to what the Democrats have already done or promised to do. They fear that by endorsing or even improving upon Democratic programs we will lose our identity as a party and appear to the world as johnny-come-lately Democrats. We will, they say, be offering an echo, not a choice.

This argument cannot be lightly dismissed. Mere imitation of Democratic programs will never make us the majority party. After a generation of vigorous, sometimes violent attacks on "the welfare state," we would look foolish if we could produce as our solutions nothing better than copies of Democratic concepts. And even if we were able to overcome the embarrassment attending such a reversal of position, we could not expect to win majorities. Were we to limit our campaigns to the claim that we *too* can plan and administer welfare programs, that would hardly convince the majority of voters to abandon the Democrats in favor of us. Republicans cannot simply out-promise the Democrats, out–New Deal the New Deal. We can suggest modifications and improvements to Democratic proposals of course — but that will not be enough to capture the political initiative or the imagination of the voters. An opposition party cannot hope to supplant the majority party simply by accepting its adversary's philosophy without adding something new and different — and at the same time, something deeply rooted in its own traditions. It must accept that part of the majority party's programs which is consistent with its principles and which has been overwhelmingly accepted by the majority of the nation in repeated elections. But it has to do more; it must go on to make its own, unique contribution. It must offer something *better.*

I am not implying that it is bad politics to accept the opposition programs when they are necessary and sound. Many Democratic programs of the past thirty-five years *have* been necessary — though less than sound in design — and we ought publicly to recognize that truth. We ought to say loudly that we too understand the needs for social security, Medicare, public housing, public health. This is said to be "me-tooism," an infamous epithet which, according to some Republicans, symbolizes all that has been wrong with the party for a generation. The charge does not intimidate me in the least. I am quite willing to say "me too" to sound solutions conceived by Democrats, and I think this harms us little, if at all. The opposite reaction — "not me!" — when unjustified, has harmed us far more. By rejecting Democratic ideas simply because they are Democratic, we may convince ourselves of our distinctive, proud identity as a party, but we also convince voters that we are more concerned with our ideology than with their problems. And we often convince them that we are rejecting the very problems themselves. To most Democratic and Independent voters, fear of "me-tooism" appears frivolous. If the opposition develops a workable, beneficial idea, much more respect is to be gained by praising and adopting it than by rejecting it summarily for fear of "copy-cat" calls. Mature leaders have always concerned themselves with the substance of issues, not whether they themselves will "look different" from competing leaders. I am convinced that "me-tooism" is less evil, and has lost us fewer votes, than our old, obsessive "not me."

But those Republicans who attack "me-tooism" relentlessly are right in one sense: it cannot serve as the foundation for a Republican revival. We need something better than the Democrats have produced, not a mere imitation of their thinking. We must offer something more useful for solving contemporary problems, more related to contemporary needs, of more meaning for most Americans. We must expose the structural flaw in the Democratic approach to solving problems — and do it without alienating the millions of voters who appreciate the constructive aspects of Democratic programs. And at the same time, we must maintain continuity with the best in the Republican past. A major party cannot simply adopt a new set of principles, ignoring all that it has represented before.

And we must make this effort not only to win votes, but also to satisfy our own desire to improve America. For we are not willing to leave the solutions of America's problems to the Democrats. Democratic leaders are, I believe, doing something fundamentally wrong. There is a flaw in the traditionally Democratic use of the powers of government. And in dealing with the problems of poverty, race and urban affairs, a traditionally Republican approach applied to present and future needs would be far superior.

I speak of a flaw in the Democratic approach to America's problems. It is a flaw so fundamental that there is some excuse for not having detected it earlier. Or, to be fair to the Democrats, a flaw so deep that it could not be recognized until the 1960's when the pressures of poverty, racial and urban problems first became intense enough to expose it. In any case, it is a major flaw, and it offers the Republican Party a superb opportunity to improve both the nation's fortunes and its own.

America's poor, her nonwhites and the inhabitants of her urban slums are linked by a common and dismal fate. Physically and psychologically, they are virtual outcasts in their own affluent society. They lack that combination of personality traits and personal qualifications essential for achievement in America. Whatever the outward symptoms of the slum, its problems in the end concern deficiencies in people, in individual men, women and children. Nothing that does not treat these deficiencies can pretend to provide permanent solutions to our problems. No governmental program, local or federal, state or county which is not directed *primarily* to overcoming personal, individual hardships can be considered effective. No subsidy, service or study that is not specifically planned to replace incompetence and fatalism with talents and aspirations can succeed.

And here is the flaw in the Democratic approach. Here is where the Democratic Party has failed. The Democrats have eased the lot of America's underprivileged minorities somewhat, but it has ignored the primary need for individual self-development. It has alleviated the misery of the patient to some degree, but it has not cured — because it has not treated — the disease. It has provided a steady, increasing dosage of aspirin instead of eliminating the source of the pain. In short, it has dealt with the symptoms of our national problems instead of the causes. And naturally it has failed, because no matter how frenzied the attempts to deal with the ever-growing symptoms — no matter how grandiose the programs planned and how huge the sums spent — the problems will continue to intensify until their causes are eliminated.

The Democrats, for example, have long championed programs of public housing and urban renewal. That is all to the good: we need public housing and urban renewal. We ought to recognize, however, that urban renewal and public housing projects are often poorly planned and administered, achieving results opposite from those intended — such as an increase in the crime rate and in the social disintegration of the neighborhood. However, that is another story, perceptively told by Jane Jacobs in *The Death and Life of American Cities.* But public housing, no matter how well designed or elaborate, is very nearly a waste of funds if not accompanied or proceeded by much greater efforts to rehabilitate the people who will occupy that housing. The ultimate cause of blighted neighborhoods is human shortcomings, not solely shabby housing. To some degree, cause and effect are intertwined: people living in poverty help deteriorate the quality of housing, and deteriorated housing helps impoverish the quality of people's lives. But surely people determine the quality of housing more than the other way around. Proof of this exists in all our cities: slums are demolished, new low-rent public housing erected, and, in a few years, the new buildings have reverted to slums, with defaced walls, broken elevators and shattered windows. By contrast, re-

sourceful families have occasionally transformed old tene-
ment houses into charming homes.

The point, I think, is obvious: slums cannot be eliminated simply by demolishing old buildings, erecting new
ones, and shifting former slum-dwellers, with their grave
lack of inner resources, from the old to the new. Unless the
cultural deficiencies of those living in slums are eliminated, public housing serves as only a temporary and
costly solution to the problem. Unless slum-dwellers are
encouraged to develop respect for property and pride in
their living quarters — pride in *themselves* — all of which
can come from a sense of dignity earned by achieving a
respected place in society — any housing they occupy
will sooner or later be transformed into a slum. Democrats
have allocated huge investments for housing; but only investment in people can lead to a lasting solution of the
"housing problem."

This misdirection of money and energy is characteristic
of almost all Democratic programs. Funds for school
lunches, tax exemptions for low incomes, federal grants for
this project and that — all these are necessary and desirable, but they cannot and do not provide permanent solutions. The Democrats, to cite another major example,
have marshaled great resources for an elaborate system of
unemployment compensation. That too is all to the good:
nothing is more tragic than a man, especially a father, who
cannot find work. Unemployment compensation is essential for relieving hardship during a temporary period
while the recently unemployed seek new work. But the
major problem is chronic unemployment, and unemployment compensation cannot solve it. It cannot solve chronic
unemployment because it does nothing to develop useful

skills and a sense of self-confidence on the part of millions of our people who are more or less permanently unemployed and virtually unemployable. To these economic outcasts, unemployment compensation could be paid forever without equipping them at all to participate actively in the give-and-take of our economy. Yet Democrats have consistently expanded compensation payments both in duration and in allotment, largely ignoring the real causes of modern unemployment and avoiding its real challenges. Giving a man temporary unemployment compensation with no concern about his ability to secure permanent employment is a grave injustice.

As much as compensation is needed to alleviate temporary suffering, in a perverse way it may prolong suffering. It is an act of mercy, a kind of charity which demonstrates compassion for those in distress, but gives them little of what they most need: the means to end the conditions that cause distress. "This kind of charity," the distinguished Trappist Father Thomas Merton has written, "has no real effect in helping the poor; all it does is tacitly to condone social injustice and to help to keep conditions as they are — to help to keep people poor." It would be unjust to say that Democrats want to keep people poor (although they do derive political advantage from keeping people on public dole), but I think it is fair to say that Democrats have done little to help dependent people to become self-supporting because they seem to have thought little about it. It is simply not in the tradition of the Democratic Party.

Or consider yet another example, the Democratic approach — at least the approach of most Democratic leaders — to the problems of racial inequality. In this decade, they have awakened to the problems at last, and promised to devote the full power and prestige of their offices to finding solutions for them. What are their solutions? They have directed their energies primarily to civil rights lawsuits, supervision of voting registration and enforcing the Civil Rights and Voting Rights Acts against segregation; in a word, to the work of the Justice Department. This too is necessary and good: Negroes everywhere in the country still suffer from unconscionable legal and ritual restrictions. We cannot call ourselves a free country until the restrictions are removed and equality of opportunity is established in fact as well as in theory. But the removal of restrictions àlone cannot hope to solve the "Negro problem." The underlying problems concern people more than laws or customs; the real task is to provide Negroes with the physical and psychological, intellectual and cultural equipment to compete with whites. Years of deprivation have left most Negroes woefully deficient in the skills and talents essential for competition. Governmental funds and energies must be directed to overcoming these deficiencies, not to making inequality more bearable. Yet the Democrats, busy with one palliative after another in the areas of housing, relief and social welfare, have failed to stimulate that human development without which all their programs, even if brilliantly executed, can only help the Negro tread water.

It would be unfair to say that Democratic administrations have wholly failed to treat our underlying national problems. Among their multitudinous, helter-skelter programs and proposals, a few have concerned themselves in a general way with education — the cornerstone of all permanent solutions. But they have never offered the nation a conscious, analytical approach to the problems of poverty, race and urban decay, an approach that would marshal the energies of government toward the goal of self-improvement. In fact they do not talk about self-improvement; they do not seem to value it. And this is why the federal government is engaged in a hundred activities to comfort the disadvantaged, spending tens of billions of dollars each year with no end in sight and no permanent results achieved.

Vice President Hubert Humphrey might be cited as representative of the prevailing attitude of liberal Democrats toward our contemporary problems. Although deeply sensitive to the crippling effects of poverty and racial injustice, Mr. Humphrey's proposals reflect obsolete thinking entirely unsuitable to this era. The Vice President, for example, suggests that every family with an income under three thousand dollars a year might be given a federal subsidy, at a total cost of eleven billion dollars a year. "Eleven billion would be a gigantic relief check," wrote Mr. Humphrey in *War on Poverty* (1964), "but it is not beyond the capacity of an American economy operating at over six hundred billion dollars a year. Certainly this nation could pay such a price, if need be, to provide a reasonable standard of living for all its citizens. A relief program of this magnitude would amount to about one-fifth of the yearly defense budget, and less than two percent of our gross national product and would be less than ten percent of our tax revenues."

I quite agree that the American economy (now nearer to seven hundred billion in gross national product than to six hundred billion) could provide eleven billion dollars in relief without serious strain. But do we need more elabo-

rate relief programs? There is something about relief —
permanent relief — that cripples the spirit and violates
the recipient's sense of honor and self-respect. It is a nega-
tion of the American Dream. And perhaps more telling, it
does not work, if by working we mean offering some promise for permanent solutions. Relief relieves desperate
pressures, but it accomplishes little or nothing toward
helping those who need it not to remain in their unfortunate condition.

I do not oppose relief. It is necessary, humane and relatively inexpensive in terms of its benefits and in terms of
our national wealth. For nonworking mothers, elderly
widows, families in distress due to sickness, unexpected
unemployment, accident or other misfortunes, relief ought
to be provided quickly and generously. But most of America's economic outcasts do not fit these categories at all.
Although potentially healthy in mind and body, they are
more or less *permanently* in distress.

If relief were the only, or the best, method of alleviating
permanent distress, I would favor it, even if it meant, to
take the most extreme example, allotting lifetime subsidies to able-bodied but unemployed young men. For a society has an obligation to provide minimum welfare for
those who cannot provide it for themselves. This is no
more than self-protection: a society containing large numbers of people who cannot make their own way is perpetu-
ally tense and potentially violent. "If the free-enterprise
system does not do its best to prevent hardship and poverty, even for those who can't be shown to deserve it," said
Senator Robert A. Taft, "it will find itself superseded by a
less progressive system which does." But this is hardly the
case in America. Relief is not the only way, not even the

best way to solve our major problems. It is costly, but more important, ineffective.

With embellishments and modifications, the Democratic approach to the paramount problems of this decade has been one of relief. Why Democrats have clung to this obsolete approach, I cannot say. Perhaps because of inertia: it is easiest to resort to the old solutions, simply doubling appropriations. Perhaps because they are confused or crippled by *their* old dogmas. During the Depression, something had gone drastically wrong with the nation's economy: the pump needed to be primed, and the New Deal measures were designed to do it. But now the country is in a quite different situation. No longer is the nation's economy as a whole beset by serious troubles — on the contrary, the pump is primed and flowing as it has never in the history of the nation; and two-thirds of our population are busy sharing its tremendous output. Now the problem is how to draw in the outcast one-third. And this will not be accomplished by old-fashioned pump-priming or other New Deal measures. But the Democratic leaders carry on in their old spirit.

Or perhaps they carry on in their old spirit for sheer political advantage. People existing on unemployment compensation, drawing pay for jobs that need not exist, supported by handouts of one sort or another are usually beholden to the Democratic Party because it is invariably the Democratic Party that provides them these supports. The supports help elect Democrats, but in the long run they are most injurious to the self-respect and the ability for self-support of the very people who are temporarily helped.

Or perhaps Democrats carry on in their old spirit because they do not fully understand or fully accept what accounts for the success of American society — and therefore what accounts for failure on the part of those who cannot compete. In both cases, it is a highly individual matter: the criteria of success or failure are intensely personal, resting on the strengths and weaknesses, skills and shortcomings, the potential for development and desire in each individual American to play the game of life well.

Unless a program is based on the understanding that American society is highly competitive, that handicaps are not given in the race for jobs and status and that success is awarded on the basis of individual accomplishment, it will always be ineffective. Unless a program is specifically designed to encourage the outcasts to engage in individual competition, it cannot be successful. But the Democrats have always been suspicious of individual enterprise. They are ill-equipped to reach the heart of our current problems — they prefer to deal with categories, groups, "general welfare" programs, rather than with the individual.

"Anticipate charity," said the twelfth-century Rabbi Moses Ben Maimon, "by preventing poverty; assist the reduced fellow man either by a considerable gift, or a sum of money, or by teaching him a trade, or by putting him in the way of business, so that he may earn an honest livelihood, and not be forced to the dreadful alternative of holding out his hand for charity." But the Democrats have not anticipated; they react after the fact — and, inevitably, too little, too late.

Whatever the causes of Democratic failure, they have been virtually relieved of censure by the even greater failure of Republican leaders to propose a satisfactory alternative. It is to the alternative we now proceed — an alternative based on individualism, in the Republican tradition.

EIGHTEEN

Helping People to Help Themselves

How ought the Republican Party to approach these problems? What should our solutions be? I believe that only an all-out, unqualified, massive attack on the conditions which doom many Americans born in disadvantaged circumstances to live their lives and rear their children in the same circumstances can promise a lasting solution. I say "massive" despite the notoriety attached to that word when used in connection with government. The problems are massive; they require massive efforts to solve them. They require a massive investment in human resources to raise the skills of disadvantaged Americans to the level of the majority — just as any backward sector of any economy requires massive investment in mechanical equipment to raise its technology to the level of world standards. The investment that normally prosperous parents ordinarily make educating themselves and their children — and which poor families, racially oppressed families, and families living in urban slums simply cannot make — must somehow be compensated for.

"No set of measures will work a perfect cure for any serious evil," said Theodore Roosevelt. No set of measures indeed will work a perfect or rapid cure for America's chronic problems. We cannot expect to find a single, quick, complete, easy solution that will supply the cultural environment — and the stability — lacking in impoverished homes. Our goal is the overcoming of those handicaps which keep the disadvantaged politically, socially and economically segregated from the rest of the nation. There is no well-marked path to that goal. On the contrary, we are setting out into uncharted territory. As one of America's World War II admirals pointed out recently, no one knew at the beginning of that war whether the submarine or the destroyer would be the more effective. Similarly, no one today knows precisely which weapons will be most effective in solving our contemporary problems.

But we should know which approach will be the most effective. We should know that giving aid and comfort without developing skills and talents promises nothing but more of the same. We must, in the spirit of a venerable but still vital Republican principle, concentrate our efforts on the individual needs of individual families living in disadvantaged circumstances.

We must, in other words, help disadvantaged Americans help themselves. In its broadest sense, it is a simple solution in theory — to help people help themselves. Republicans have talked in these terms for decades. They have become tired words, and I am afraid that many Americans think they are clichés. But they represent a sound principle, the only principle that is relevant to long-term solutions to America's problems. *Our* problem, as Republicans, is simply to convince the country that this principle can work and then to make it work. It cannot work — in fact, the principle is discredited — if we do no more than intone pious phrases and fond hopes. It will work if *we* work to apply the principle to specific needs of specific people faced with specific problems.

To help people help themselves, we must in the first place remove the obstacles in our national life which tend to keep the poor, racially oppressed and slum-dwellers where they are. In other words, we must seek out the flaws in the *system* which tend to perpetuate poverty, segregation and slums. We must tear down the barriers in our social, political and economic institutions that help keep Americans disadvantaged instead of helping them break free of their disadvantages.

There are a great number of institutional reforms which the Republican Party could sponsor and support to help underprivileged people help themselves. Increasing the minimum wage, for example, would bring some immediate benefits. According to Herman Miller, an expert on poverty statistics in the Bureau of Census, "about fifty percent of [the poor] are in families headed by a full-time worker whose wages are simply too low to support a family." But a higher minimum wage is often less important than extending the existing minimum to cover workers unprotected by minimum wage legislation. For example, hospital workers, unskilled restaurant help and unskilled retail workers who earn fifty dollars or less a week are, if they are raising a family, almost certainly doomed to poverty even if they are working full time. The paradox we observe then is that many of the families who most need the protection of minimum wage laws are excluded from them. Skilled industrial workers and others whose wages are far above the minimum are protected, but many working in jobs paying much less than the minimum are not.

The same applies to unemployment insurance. It is estimated that as many as two out of five workers in the American labor force are not covered by the federal-state unemployment insurance system. It is often argued that unemployment insurance should be increased. Perhaps that is necessary in many states. But far more important is the expansion of the system to include those workers who will most likely suffer chronic or seasonal unemployment — to include those who most need protection, but are now excluded from it.

Recent statistics indicate that a fifth of the total of America's poor are aged. In their case, a simple addition to their income, even a small addition in percentage terms, would go far toward alleviating distress.

Relief payments too must be increased where relief is needed. For in most states the level of relief is appallingly low — it is the difference between the applicant's resources (plus the resources of his legally responsible relatives) and a minimum standard set by the state. But these minimum standards are often themselves below the poverty level. (New York's relatively liberal welfare grants, for example, average twenty-five per cent below the estimated poverty level.) They do not allow the families involved to make the investment in education and training for themselves and their children necessary to break free from poverty.

Nor are our present medical services adequate to meet the needs of those living in oppressed circumstances. The incidence of sickness, chronic disease, and debilitating illness is significantly greater among the poor whites and nonwhites than among other Americans. In fact, blindness or other physical disabilities are often the cause of poverty. Many of the chronically poor, weakened by an improper diet over an extended period, develop chronic diseases, and these diseases in turn help keep them poor. Where medical care, both preventive and curative, is most needed, it is difficult to obtain. The poor need far more medical help than most Americans, and they get far less. Medicare, although essential, comes too late in life to help the poor during their best working years. Either the benefits of Medicare must be extended to younger people in need or effective measures must be taken to insure that there are private medical services adequate for their needs.

The simplest kind of reform in terms of government intervention in the economy would be a revision of tax laws to ease the burden in lower-income brackets. Another of the paradoxes in our economic life is that families living below the poverty line pay part — albeit a small part — of their income for taxes even though this expenditure often, in the long run, costs the government more than it takes in. Even the small sum that these families must pay in taxes represents a severe strain on the family's ability to provide itself with the essentials of food, clothing and medical care. As a result, government, at one level or another, must fill the gap — and often a greater gap than would have existed were the tax payment abated. Not enough milk and meat in the diet means sickness and unemployment; not enough money for shoes means children do not go to school. In the end, the government pays more to correct these defects than it collects in taxes from the people who suffer them. Economically as well as morally, therefore, it makes sense to give more generous tax benefits to poor families and especially to the aged and the widowed.

A "reverse" or "negative" income tax ought to be seriously considered as a means of raising income of the disadvantaged to an established minimum level. Once, this idea was considered revolutionary. But now, based on the fact that the potential exemptions of many poor families exceed their incomes, it appears more and more logical. In other words, the father of a family of six who earns $3000 a year and has exemptions totalling $3600 for that year, thus incurring no tax liability, would receive $600 from the federal government, which is the amount of his total exemptions over and above his total income. The $600 would be paid by a federal appropriation or from "found money" — money collected by the Internal Revenue in interest and penalties for late payment of income taxes. If this sounds like outlandish charity, it ought to be remembered that such a family often costs the local, state and federal government far more than $600 in that year in terms of welfare services. Such a direct payment might in fact be simpler, more effective and more economical. We grant special tax exemptions to many individuals and businesses in special circumstances — such as the depletion allowance given to the petroleum industry as an incentive to find more oil. Why not use our tax laws to combat the special circumstances of poverty — as a form of assistance to the oppressed to help themselves.

Measures to increase the rate of our economic growth would also be helpful for those living on the fringes of our economy. For although economic growth is not a cure-all for eliminating poverty as it was once assumed, nevertheless, it is an essential weapon in the arsenal of antipoverty measures. A full-employment economy would immediately help those of the poor who live in families whose heads are unemployed or partially unemployed. More funds invested in new plants, new machinery and new public works projects will create new jobs and new opportunities. And while new jobs cannot help those who are unemployed because they are sick or untrained, unless they exist all the educational and medical services in the world are wasted. In other words, a high rate of economic growth with increased production and increased demand is essential in the war against poverty.

Another essential weapon is the elimination of all remaining racial restrictions, both legal and traditional. For nonwhites comprise roughly twenty-five per cent of the nation's poor, and an even greater percentage of the chronically poor. No series of programs that does not liberate nonwhites from their disadvantages can eradicate the causes of poverty.

All of these measures and others to correct institutional flaws in our system can be valuable. But they cannot be valuable without planning — particularly long-range planning. The most successful American businesses use planning together with experimentation of new techniques in a remarkably effective way. The government must learn to imitate business in this respect. Study and planning for the specific needs of specific individuals who are segregated racially, economically and culturally are not an excuse to avoid action. Study and planning are an absolute prerequisite for any kind of intelligent action.

The Democrats have struck out in every possible direc-

tion without the elementary planning which constitutes
the required first step for any kind of successful program,
governmental or nongovernmental. We are now witnessing
under a Democratic administration a proliferation of
agencies and a potpourri of antipoverty programs which
were thrown together slapdash and bear no resemblance
to a coordinated, controlled, step-by-step series of actions
that would constitute an authentic war on poverty. In
fact, present programs, far from being coordinated, appear to be operated in competition with one another, as if
the real war were among federal, state and local agencies, instead of against poverty. Each agency — and
there are literally dozens of them — seems determined to
"grab a piece" of a poor family and hang onto it, struggling to enhance its own power and prestige by proving
its approach is best. As with so many programs sponsored
by the Democratic Party, the emphasis has been on protecting the institutions and their prerogatives, rather than
the individuals that the institutions are created to serve.

We have embarked on a war which America cannot afford to lose — yet embarked on it ill-prepared, ill-
equipped and ill-led. The cause is simply too important to
allow its implementation to be left in incompetent hands.
We need organization, skillful and humane administration, modern accounting techniques and, above all, we
need *plans*. We need blueprints drawn by experts — by
people appointed on the basis of professional expertise, not
political patronage. The Republican Party should take
the opportunity afforded by the obvious deficiencies in
Democratic implementation to come forth with a care-
fully researched, logically developed master plan. Let us
offer the kinds of skills in planning and administration

that Republicans have in abundance. For the war on poverty desperately needs those Republican skills.

The first obligation, then, of the Republican Party in helping the disadvantaged to help themselves is to conduct a searching examination of how our social, economic and political institutions affect the disadvantaged. It must suggest ways which, taken together with a planned, coordinated set of measures, would facilitate the movement of disadvantaged people into the mainstream of American life. Institutional reforms enabling the disadvantaged to invest in themselves will quickly pay significant rewards. The family with a little more income, a little more security, a little better medical care, a little greater interaction with the currents of "normal America" will be able to make a much greater effort to help itself.

But we cannot limit ourselves to removing the institutional barriers restricting the underprivileged. We must give them direct help which is channeled toward self-development. Helping the poor and the racially oppressed to help themselves requires a direct investment in the human resources they represent. For even if the institutional barriers were removed, they do not now have the ability to help themselves. And without the help of the nation as a whole, they cannot acquire that ability.

Helping people acquire the ability to help themselves must be the essence of the Republican approach.

The ability to help oneself is dependent primarily upon a variety of sources. But surely the principle source is education. Only education can break the heritage of disadvantage and defeatism now systematically handed down from generation to generation. Only education, understood in its broadest sense, can overcome the competitive disadvantages bequeathed the underprivileged and equip them to make their own way in a free-enterprise system.

This might seem too obvious to bear emphasizing were it not for the fact that as a nation we are failing pitifully to discharge our educational obligations. While it may be important to produce swift halfbacks, and while it may be important to induce in our youngsters an unconscious attitude of adjustment, it seems much more important to imbue in all our students the ability to think. While a knowledge of current events and the ability to comprehend *TV Guide* may serve our youngsters, it would appear that much more important is a stretching of the mind — a desire to expand and grope in unknown areas. Surely, though, we can never redo our public school system without rethinking our total approach to education which, by necessity, has to include at the starting point our approach to the teachers themselves. Underpaid and overvacationed, the teaching profession on the elementary and secondary levels should be attracting to it more individuals who are gifted, who are intellectuals and who are creative and industrious — qualities that are absolutely essential if we are to "progress" as a nation in any real sense of the word.

We need to consider the total problem of education, including the way it has been arbitrarily charted. We need to consider the best use of children's formative years. We may even need to use teachers differently and to teach different types of things in different ways. One recent development which I feel teachers are not utilizing as they should is the so-called Paperback Revolution. Although in this year 1966 it may seem odd that our education system is still struggling along with the established and usually unexciting textbook anthologies, that, nevertheless, is the case. It should seem clear even to the most muddled school administrator that the world's best literature is now available at low prices and it would follow that all school systems must adjust to the development of the paperback. But, of course, the educational system will not adjust until, as a profession, more individuals of high quality are drawn into the ranks.

We have been clinging to a traditionally designed educational system. As an example, the nine-month school period and the three-month vacation period is a heritage from our agricultural past which does not characterize our country at the present time. The children who were excused from school in the summer months to work on the farm do not work on the farm any more. And the great majority of them are unable to find jobs. What should be done with their time? How can their time best be used to improve their minds and bodies?

The educational facilities of the nation are poorest precisely where they should be best. Two out of three unemployed American workers lack a high school education. In Harlem, 80 per cent of sixth grade students are below sixth grade norms; almost all high school students in Harlem are below standard norms — eleven out of twenty are unable to graduate. It has been estimated that 50 per cent to 75 per cent of slum children are failing to get a minimal high school education in our public school system. In Cook County, Illinois, 85 per cent of those receiving welfare aid did not graduate from high school and the national figure may be as high as 90 per cent. In terms of preparing disadvantaged children to make use of American opportunity, our educational resources are sadly underdeveloped.

Nothing can reverse this trend except a vast educational program that will give the disadvantaged a fighting chance to catch up. Since their domestic environment is inferior to that of "normal" Americans, their schools must be made not equal to, but *better than* the average schools. Since they are discouraged from competing for the Good Life almost from the moment of birth, they must be encouraged by educators to work not as hard, but *harder*. Since they have been subjected to poorer cultural influences throughout their childhood, they must be given exposure to cultural influences which are not equal, but *richer*.

I would prefer not to become involved in debating whether giving *more* to the children of the poor and racially oppressed is "fair." That question is philosophically interesting. But it has no more relevance to the practical solution of our problems than the question of whether our treatment of the poor and racially oppressed has been "fair" in the past. Probably both are "unfair" according to philosophical and ethical criteria; probably the unfairness of centuries of deprivation far outweigh the unfairness of providing unequal allocations for education over the next two or three generations.

But I am not suggesting vast government expenditure in education merely to balance one unfairness with another, or to square an old debt. There is no satisfactory way to right past wrongs of this sort, or to redeem past debts to past generations.

My point is simply that no other approach will solve our problems in this and future generations. Talk of fairness or unfairness avoids the real issue. Only by investing more in education in the next few generations can we avoid spending far more for doles in perpetuity. Massive improvement in our educational system is the only effective approach and it will be the cheapest approach in the long run. Obviously we cannot expect that private funds and foundations can cope with a problem of this magnitude. Much as we would like the elimination of poverty to be a private affair, such a thought is utopian.

We need an educational program of major proportions. Measured in terms of the needs, President Johnson's poverty program is pitifully inadequate and misdirected. At best, it is a rearguard action in a losing cause. To make ours a winning cause, the people trapped in slums must be provided with grammar and high school education, vocational education and adult education far beyond anything yet proposed by either political party. In other words, our local educational systems must be strengthened by great infusions of funds and expertise. But local educational systems, themselves often stultified by the effects of poverty, are not enough. A national educational training corps staffed by thousands of professional teachers — paid substantial premiums to work in slum areas, just as soldiers are paid premiums for combat duty — must be established with the specific goal of eliminating the "educational gap." Such a corps could serve during a period of transition while we rethink and retool our total approach to education. In short, we Republicans must declare war on educational deficiency, and we must wage it with the same energy, efficiency and willingness to spend money with which the Cold War is waged. No single campaign or series of campaigns will be satisfactory.

We must commit ourselves to a protracted war in which victory will mean the growth and development of young people, with roughly the same talents, qualifications and ambitions, regardless of where they happen to live or the color of their skin. Nothing less than this promises success. Obviously, investment and dedication are required on a scale never before approached in American public education.

But I do not mean education simply in terms of books and teachers. The effects of poverty, particularly of cultural poverty, cannot be alleviated in schools alone. Recent studies have shown that by the time they reach kindergarten, most disadvantaged children are already severely handicapped to the extent that catching up in school is exceedingly difficult. Much of the traditional school curriculum is wasted on them because they are psychologically and culturally unprepared to learn. The traditional school curriculum bears little relationship to what they have learned in their preschool years and to what they observe in their parents and envisage for their own futures.

Education is not simply learning. Its first task is instilling the attitudes and self-confidence that makes learning possible. It means developing an intangible psychological attitude toward the world, an attitude that liberates a child's potential to develop, rather than smothering it. For the children of the poor and of the racial ghettos, school must start at age three or four in order to develop in them a cultural interest, an awareness of beauty, an awareness of themselves and an awareness of their potential. It is necessary that education begin early in the formative years before these children are stunted permanently by the disadvantages of a culturally deprived home environment. This is absolutely essential for any program of self-development and self-generating growth. And this must be the philosophy of the Republican approach to these problems. The Republican Party must take the leadership in giving to underprivileged children the eagerness to learn, the will to learn and the hope that they can learn. For without these, they cannot learn.

I suggest therefore that we establish a comprehensive system of preschool centers operating both during the school year and in the summer for the children of the underprivileged. These should be well-equipped, full-time institutions staffed by trained, well-paid teachers and child psychologists.

Operation Headstart represents a beginning, but only a hesitant first step. The operation must be vastly expanded, systematized, and imaginatively administered. It must be integrated into a solid system, rather than a temporary, makeshift arrangement operating here and lacking there.

These preschool centers would not provide the beginnings of a formal education, but they would provide something much more essential at that age: the sense of self and security which is a prerequisite to successful formal education. They would provide a social community, which would afford the underprivileged children an opportunity to meet other children in a healthy atmosphere. And most important, they would provide sympathetic adults to listen to them and to encourage them to develop their potential for self-expression.

That the mind of a child is elastic and will stretch beyond all comprehension has been established. For verification we need only look at the MacDowell experiment in Stamford, Connecticut, where children of preschool age demonstrate amazing creativity and perceptiveness through their use of machines such as typewriters. The proof is irrefutable that the mind is indeed an amazing system of responses and creations. The mind feeds on challenge, and it is challenge that our public school system, in many instances, does not provide.

I have been told recently of some experiments in child psychology being conducted in New York. Children from impoverished and others from middle-class homes were shown a series of pictures. One picture, for example, showed a red bicycle with white stripes. The children were asked, "Is the bicycle white?" Almost without exception, those from impoverished homes answered in a single word, "No." But the children from middle-class homes went on to exercise their powers of speech, reasoning and imagination. "No, it's not white — it's red but only striped with white. If you wanted it all red you could get my daddy to paint it. My sister has a red bicycle, but it's got more white."

In another example, the children were shown a picture of a tree with a single apple hanging from a branch, and dozens scattered near the trunk. "Are the apples on the tree?" both groups were asked. Again, almost invariably, the children from impoverished homes answered simply, "No." But the middle-class children went on to explain at some length, "No, there is only one apple on the tree. The rest are on the ground. If you wait, maybe the other apple will fall too. Or you could get a ladder and knock it down. I once saw an apple tree . . ."

The psychologists conclude that the overwhelming majority of children from disadvantaged homes have never been encouraged to develop their imaginations or ability of expression. On the contrary, the disadvantaged children are led to believe that their opinions are not valuable and not wanted. But the middle-class children, even at ages three and four, have already developed a self-confidence, imagination and ability to communicate, and a sense of the value of communication. They have already begun the process of learning and expressing.

This is what the preschool centers can help provide. They can offer disadvantaged children a feeling of contact with the world, a sense of what they *can* do, a taste of life, of excitement, of beauty. They can whet their appetites and stimulate their aspirations. They can encourage a discontent with the life to which disadvantaged children had previously been exposed. And they can help to bring about an unwillingness by those children to be restricted to slums and ghettos.

While I have been primarily discussing education for the poor, I think that the problem of education applies across the board through our entire society. Our public school system is inadequate and I feel that education is so important to the growth of our nation and, indeed, to the mental health of our people that the Republican Party should propose the immediate establishment of a federal department whose total commitment is to education. When we consider the many existing departments of our federal government, it is tragic that education, which is of paramount concern and which underlies everything including the very principles of democratic government, has not achieved individual departmental status. We cannot begin to build any meaningful programs without presupposing concomitant programs aimed at educating all of America as best we can, as well as specifically educating the poor and the disadvantaged.

America's dismally poor, underprivileged nonwhites and inhabitants of slums are the avoided Americans. They are seldom, if ever, seen by advantaged Americans. With the exception of professionals, suppliers and service personnel who must by necessity go into their sectors of life, they are shunned, circled and bypassed. The barriers that contain them are public and private, real and psychological, legal and illegal. In most cases, the doctor, lawyer, clergyman, teacher, policeman, and even social worker no longer lives among them. At the close of the business day, all return to their homes, which are usually outside of the impoverished sector. The underprivileged are then left to go it alone. But racial oppression and the problems of poverty and slums do not stop at the close of day. If anything, they increase and intensify. It is then, more than at any other time, that discontent, unrest, resentment and bitterness mount. It is then, when stripped of their link with the outside world, that the disadvantaged are plagued by hopelessness and despair. There is no one to whom they can turn for help. They are shut up and shut out. The normal communication media are alien to them. Some cannot read, or if they can, they neither read nor comprehend substantive materials in newspapers or periodicals. For those few who have acquired television or radio, they neither watch nor understand the few substantive programs offered.

How then can these Americans be reached? How can they be helped to help themselves? What vehicle is best for the kind of work needed for developing aspirations, attitudes and personal habits essential for their moral, spiritual, intellectual and economic improvement? Obviously, present solutions can hardly be considered successful. And obviously, a different, if not new, approach to the problems is needed.

What then do the underprivileged need to help them improve themselves?

They need jobs. For the real source of poverty is lack of jobs. The poor have been told that the blame is theirs because they lack the necessary skills. The fact is that even if the poor possessed the necessary skills there are still too few skilled jobs available. The poor have been criticized for not wanting work. The fact is that the poor have literally swamped employment agencies with applications for unskilled and semiskilled jobs.

Here, the Republican Party should propose ways to produce more skilled, semiskilled and unskilled jobs through more enterprising use of the public and private sectors of the nation's economy. For example, the Republican Party should propose a return to more frequent daily mail deliveries, which would open up thousands of new jobs. In addition, the Republican Party should propose a massive clean-up-and-beautify-America program which would also create thousands of unskilled jobs.

The poor need consumer protection. They have precious little buying power and when they are able to buy, they are confronted with inferior products, the highest interest rates and ingenious credit traps. They are usually unaware of interest, carrying charges and penalties they are obliged to pay. And they have little or no education in thrift and investment.

Here, the Republican Party should propose protective

consumer legislation which will limit the *true* interest rate that the consumer can be charged and provide for mandatory disclosure of the *actual* prices and finance charges on installment sales' contracts. The proposed legislation should prohibit certain practices now permitted that are burdensome and unfair to the nation's consumers, such as the use of acceleration clauses which make the entire principal on an installment sale come due even though there has been no serious breach of the contract by the buyer; the "balloon payment," a final payment considerably in excess of the previous installments which the purchaser has made; confession of judgment clauses; and provisions for exorbitant refinancing charges. In addition, the Republican Party should propose legislation that would provide the consumer with thrift and investment education through the media of printed material, radio and television.

And the disadvantaged need people, people from advantaged America who are willing to live among them and work with them, people who are not so much a part of a profession but a part of a calling — a calling to work among and with the poor, racially oppressed and inhabitants of slums. In addition, the underprivileged need the opportunity to be heard as well as to be advised — the opportunity to participate at the policy level formulating policy as to how they, themselves, can best be helped.

To help the nation's disadvantaged help themselves, the Republican Party should propose a federally supported program for the reactivation of the ideas originally embodied in the settlement-house movement. Such a program would help to develop harmonious relationships among community groups with various religious, cultural, economic and social characteristics. Neighborhoods would be developed by getting people to act together, to be informed and to improve their living conditions. The underprivileged would acquire a sense of belonging, a sense of identity and a sense that someone cares. And the causes of hardship would be removed by the improvement of the neighborhood through interaction.

Self-help has always been a cherished Republican principle. The problems facing the avoided Americans offer the Republican Party an opportunity to match principle with program.

America's great urban centers present many more problems than poverty, racial oppression and slums with which the Republican Party must come to grips. City streets are clogged with traffic and city transit systems are becoming more and more inefficient. City parks and recreation space are rapidly disappearing. City schools and hospitals are overcrowded and obsolete. City air is polluted by exhaust fumes and industrial smoke. City water supplies are threatened with contamination through unnecessary pollution of streams and rivers. These problems are the product of economic and social forces within our society which cannot be effectively controlled by the individual alone. The initiative and ultimate responsibility for them must remain at the local level, but our cities simply cannot finance them without support from the federal government. Needed to meet the crisis in our cities is a viable and dynamic partnership, a sharing of resources, between all levels of government. The Republican Party should support relief from the federal government for the spreading costs of local expenditures. Governor William Scranton of Pennsylvania has succinctly outlined a sound Republican approach to this problem. "How much better would it be if the Republican Party would implement a legislative program that recognized that though the Federal Government has the tax resources, local governments are often far more capable of using the money efficiently and effectively."

As I have suggested, the cities are now incapable of coping effectively with these problems and are becoming less and less capable. As these problems mount and as the city centers swell with the people living in poverty, and the costs of welfare services rise, the taxpayers of the central cities are shrinking. Nor are state governments capable of coping with the problems. There is little in the inherent structure of state governments that prevents them from enacting corrective programs, but in fact few legislatures have been willing to face the problems of their own cities. The reasons are political. Most state legislatures are dominated by rural interests which mitigate against a serious attack on city problems. And tax raising in most states is a highly political, highly delicate matter. We are left therefore with the federal government. There is no alternative.

Other grave problems include the nation's high school dropouts, who will number about eight million by 1970 if the trend is not reversed. Here, the Republican Party should support vocational training programs.

The shortage of doctors, nurses and dentists for the care and treatment of the nation's sick and infirm is expanding. Here, the Republican Party should support federal aid for the construction of medical schools and legislation for the establishment of a self-liquidating scholarship loan fund so that qualified students in financial need can receive quality training.

Mental illness is the nation's number one health problem, affecting millions of our citizens and their families. Public outlays in the area of mental illness and mental retardation are over 2.4 billion dollars a year, but we have only begun to deal with the causes and cures for these problems. Here, the Republican Party should support legislation which would broaden research, modernize deteriorated facilities and bring more manpower to bear on this crucial health problem.

Although urban renewal has changed the face of some of the nation's cities for the better, the social problems behind the new physical faces have too often remained the same — important human factors have been neglected. Neighborhoods, in the true sense of the word, have been destroyed and families uprooted. Too many projects have not been properly planned. Others have been thoughtlessly and callously executed. Some of the areas chosen for clearance are precisely those which show the most promise of making a comeback on their own. Justifiable complaints have been raised about the demolition of structurally sound buildings. But that objection pales when compared to the destruction of the character of city neighborhoods by literally driving out long-time residents. Once an area has been chosen for redevelopment, building improvement usually stops, thus accelerating the very blight it was intended to cure. And this problem has been compounded by the fact that there have been delays of more than five or six years from the time when planning begins and blueprints are drawn to the completion of the projects.

But the crucial and most devastating indictment of urban renewal is that too often it causes a loss of communal feeling and strips communities of their unique flavor, their warmth, their esprit, as well as their physical buildings — churches, men's clubs, corner grocery stores and teen-age meeting places. And in far too many cases, low-income and minority families have been displaced only to find that the price tag on the proffered new housing in the "renewed" neighborhood or a new neighborhood of their choice was just too high. The result: a disappearance into other slums or areas soon to become slums.

It has been estimated that a million families will be displaced by urban renewal during the next decade. Half that number will be Negro families. And although urban renewal has been hailed as a positive tool to decongest Negro ghettos, in practice, urban renewal and racial discrimination have often gone hand in hand.

What is needed is not an abandonment of urban renewal. The concept is a sound one. The need exists.

But, here, the Republican Party has an opportunity to propose a humane and well-administered program of urban renewal, together with an enlightened program of conservation and rehabilitation of existing structures. The emphasis should be placed on the inhabitant, on his relocation and on the revitalization of existing buildings and communities. This must be augmented by encouraging private investment in urban renewal and encouraging increased interest on the part of private agencies. This Republicans can do and must do.

The federal government in cooperation with state governments is in the process of building an immense federal highway system. That is good for a growing country and a travel-oriented people. It is also good that the nation's air and bus travel facilities are expanding rapidly. But all of these are hardly able to accommodate the ever-increasing number of those who travel throughout the country or those who transport the nation's products from place to place.

Here, the Republican Party should propose a giant transportation network that would include the airplane, a revitalized passenger train, the bus and the urban-suburban mass transportation systems. Such a program should be under a federal department of transportation utilizing the best technical and administrative abilities available. Ownership and control should remain in private transportation companies. The role of the federal department of transportation should be limited to integration and coordination. Air, bus, train and rapid-transit terminals should be integrated into a giant network. The system should be safe, fast, convenient and comfortable. A traveler who boards a rapid-transit train in a suburb of San Francisco, California, should be able to arrive at his destination in Quincy, Massachusetts, without having to travel on a national highway or a city or suburban street. The result would be vastly improved transportation for the nation's passengers and cargo, instant mobility in time of local and national emergency, relief for the nation's congested highways, and, as a by-product, more jobs for the nation's unemployed. Again, no city or state has the financial resources to solve the problem, and as in so many other problem areas, the answer lies in a city-state-national partnership.

These problems are complex and interwoven. They require action at many levels. To solve them will require imagination, research, planning and the cooperation of private organizations, community, state and federal governments. The Republican Party should take the lead in federal-local arrangements to meet these problems — new economic arrangements that would allow more money to be returned to the states which have a high administrative capacity but a low fiscal capacity such as tax credit, sharing of tax base and a continuation and augmentation of grant-in-aid programs.

All of the programs that I have suggested for Republican Party sponsorship cost money. And as it should be, we Republicans always ask where is the money to come from? First, we must face the fact that no offensive against poverty, racial oppression, slums, and the myriad of other problems can succeed without increasing expenditures. But let me make one thing absolutely clear. We are not going to lose money or weaken America's economic system by helping in the solution of these problems. No group will suffer — not the middle class, the upper class, or the working class. On the contrary, the chronically poor will get richer, but so will everyone else. Every American will benefit economically as well as morally.

An allout effort to help the disadvantaged to join the mainstream of American life would be one of the wisest and most profitable investments in our national history. It was estimated in 1963 that the 35 million Americans living in poverty had a total aggregate income of some 12 billion dollars below the estimated requirements for a minimally comfortable standard of living. On the other hand, it was also estimated that some 30 to 40 billion dollars was lost to the American economy in buying power because these 35 million disadvantaged remained outside the normal economic life of the nation. Clearly, an investment to bring these people into the mainstream — as buyers and suppliers of every kind of goods and services — will pay enormous rewards. It will add at least 30 billion dollars each year to the gross national product — and more, as the skills, and with these the buying power, of the now-disadvantaged increase. And this, of course, speaks only of the financial rewards. The real return must be measured in terms of human lives.

The money for the federal programs would come from increased spending by the federal government and increased spending would be expected to increase the gross national product. Increased national income would come from expanded productivity and tax revenues out of the increased national income would service the debt. This would mean an increase in income taxes but it would also mean more of an increase in income. The debt created would be an internal debt which the American people would owe to each other. They would pay the taxes and receive the interest on the debt.

This is not a simple or painless way to finance our proposed programs. I believe there are no simple or painless ways. It will require a large expenditure of government funds. It will mean new efforts in the "public sector" of our economy. I think there is no other way to reach our goals. The economic historian Robert Heilbroner writing in the *Saturday Review* put these matters in perspective in a recent survey of America's needs: "This is not to say," he wrote, "that the sphere of private wants will not grow or that the private sector will not remain dominant in our economic life. But the challenge of the future no longer lies in the private zone. It is the public zone that is still small and mean and dingy and poor — and increasingly important. Here is where the horizons are big."

No one wants to commit the federal government unnecessarily to new programs and expenditures. In the best of all possible worlds, it would not be necessary. In contemporary America, postponing action will cause greater inconvenience, expense, and danger than would bold massive action.

Consider the alternatives. Unless substantial gains, or at least realistic hope for substantial gains, are achieved soon, America will continue to be plagued by demonstrations, bitterness, violence — or the fear of them. We will continue to witness pickets marching on our main streets, chaining themselves to our City Halls, and sitting at White House entrances, and continue to experience the humiliation, the *shame,* caused not primarily by these spectacles but by the conditions which inspire them. We will continue to suffer the tensions which these conditions produce in American life, and all the effects of this — steadily intensifying — tension. How long? As long as the problems exist. Are we willing to suffer these effects for a decade, two decades, a century?

We will continue to spend huge monthly sums for welfare payments, relief payments and other measures which, by nature, can solve nothing but only supply a minimum of temporary and expensive relief. Are we willing to keep sending our children to schools whose standards are lowered by children raised in material and cultural poverty? Or to keep paying large tuition fees at private schools to escape that necessity? Are we willing to keep enduring the disastrous side-effects of poverty and discrimination such as crime, illegitimacy, and wasted human and economic potential? (No one has calculated the total costs of these side-effects in dollars, but surely it is many times greater annually than the total cost for a massive ten-year program of reeducation. It costs the taxpayers of New York, for example, $7000 to raise a single child on relief to the age of seventeen.) Are we willing to keep paying for the poor and the racially disadvantaged in a hundred ways, to keep living side by side with ugliness, ignorance, cynicism and resentment?

These are the alternatives. As much as we might hope for others, I believe there are none. There is a great deal we do not like about the "other" America, a great deal to which we would prefer not to subject ourselves and our children. But these things will not disappear by themselves; on the contrary, left alone or treated haphazardly as they have been treated, they can only intensify. We are going to pay more and more relief for unwed mothers living in the slums; we are going to pay greater and greater sums to battle — less and less effectively — urban crime.

We are deeply disturbed by these aspects of American life, but we cannot wish them away. Our national life will continue to be disturbed until we commit ourselves to eliminating them — in the only realistic way possible, by eliminating the sources, something which the Democratic Party historically has failed to do.

The Republican Party has traditionally felt that the principal function of government is helping people to help themselves. Now it has the opportunity to discharge that function on a scale unprecedented in American history. We have traditionally believed in investing funds wisely rather than spending profusely for projects which offer no promise of return. And now we have an opportunity for investment in the future of the country which will not only give a dollar's value for a dollar spent, but is also guaranteed to produce enormous profits. We have traditionally argued that the Democrats have temporized and faltered, rushing from one expedient welfare measure to the next because they do not fully understand the nature of America's problems. Now the opportunity is ours to demonstrate an understanding of the real issues confronting the nation and to offer lasting solutions rather than everlasting subsidies. We have traditionally believed that individual initiative made America great, and that governmental programs which sabotage initiative are in the long run self-perpetuating or self-defeating. We have recognized that America has thrived on differences and that the American melting pot was never intended to produce a bland gruel-like American who thinks like his neighbor, looks like his neighbor and talks and acts like his neighbor; that it was never intended to blur the complexity, the diversity, or the wonder of difference in Americans. And we have led the fight against the repression of individuality and difference by conformity — conformity of dress, conformity of art, conformity of activity and the resulting great danger, conformity of thought. And now we have an opportunity to really protect individualism by encouraging individual effort on the part of tens of millions of Americans who are now capable of woefully little of it.

The Democrats are known as great theorizers and great idealists, but they seldom follow through in any measure relative to their basic idealism. Already the present Democratic administration has begun to hedge on its concept of the Great Society. President Johnson has encountered

[213]

considerable difficulty in finding competent hard-nosed administrators for his programs. No matter what the administration speeches and press releases say, the President has already begun to retreat from his commitments to domestic solutions, giving as the reason, the growing burden of Vietnam. The reason is understandable and I don't think that anyone who believes in our commitment in Vietnam is going to object to the President's cutting back on his Great Society to honor that commitment. But from a vantage point of hindsight, President Johnson should have recognized that as the Vietnam war began to escalate, his Great Society would never be able to get under way with any great effect so long as he was determined to employ the vast amount of resources which he has employed in Vietnam. The assumption from all of this is that the Johnson administration has played politics as usual, promising everything to everybody and forgetting the hard realities which face the nation.

It is also surmisable that due to a lack of administrative ability and business tenacity within the Johnson administration, the President's proposed expenditures and programs may never ever get back into daylight.

I fully realize that in the area of foreign affairs any administration, Republican or Democratic, will constantly have to alter certain domestic expenditures for international commitments. But what the nation needs in this crucial moment in our history is administrative strength and business tenacity which, though pursuing an intelligent foreign policy, will keep a constant vigil on domestic policies and expenditures and as a result see vital domestic programs to fruition.

A Republican Party, which will not forget reality and

which will draw upon its hard business training and administrative follow-through, is best equipped to solve our complex national problems. It is time for the Republican Party to act. For these are times when cursing the darkness has become unacceptable to the vast majority of American people. The vast majority is waiting for us to strike the match.

NINETEEN

✣ ✣ ✣

Responsibility in Foreign Policy

WHEN America's security and prosperity are profoundly affected by daily events in Peru, Pakistan,
Tanzania and a hundred other countries, the Republican
Party can succeed only by offering responsible leadership
for the conduct of foreign affairs.

It is not necessarily true that solutions to our domestic
problems always, or even ordinarily, bear any relationship
to solutions to our foreign problems. But at the present
time that happens to be the case. It happens to be the
case, logically enough, because certain of our underlying
foreign and domestic problems are strikingly similar. We
have seen that the gap between the prosperous majority of
Americans and the underprivileged minority is widening.
Precisely this process is taking place in the world at large.
But in the world at large, the overwhelming majority is
poor — poorer than most Americans can imagine. And the
difficulties the poor of the world face in attaining even the
lowest level of American poverty are staggering.

In a sense, the world's population divides itself into two
categories: a relatively small minority which has excellent
prospects for building a reasonably comfortable, se-

cure and satisfying life; and the great majority which has almost no such prospects. Outside of North America and Europe, a few outposts of prosperity like Australia, Israel and Japan, and to a lesser extent the Soviet Union, life for most of the world's people is a grim, relentless struggle for daily bread. These are the inhabitants of the underdeveloped nations, which are becoming steadily poorer relative to the rich nations, and in some cases poorer in terms of per capita income. They are predominantly nonwhite, and in a sense, they live in vast ghettos, bypassed by the soaring increase of wealth and technical expertise produced in the rich nations. Often they cannot sustain enough economic growth to match the growth in their populations — to say nothing of achieving the enormous economic growth necessary for genuine progress.

The quality of a people's life cannot be measured accurately in terms of economic statistics alone, but statistics do help describe the physical misery endured by most people in most of the underdeveloped world. The contrast with even the lowest American standards is appalling. Per capita income in America is over $2500 a year, and increasing rapidly; in two-thirds of the world, per capita income is under $200 a year — and hardly increasing at all. Since 1960 American per capita income has *increased* by more than $250 — which is roughly equal to the *total* per capita income in (to pick a significant example) the Dominican Republic. (To cite another significant example, per capita income in South Vietnam was estimated at $120 in 1965.) And the average per capita income in all Latin American countries together is not significantly greater: roughly $300 a year.

But three hundred dollars represents magical wealth

to half the world's people. Five hundred million people in India, for example, live on less than seventy dollars per person a year. Admittedly the cost of living in India is significantly lower than it is in the United States, but still the comparison is disturbingly valid. The same $70 per year would purchase only $300 worth of goods and services at American prices — an almost negligible buying power in our country where the government has established that any annual family income of less than $3000 is substandard.

How can the plight of the two billion impoverished people of the world be described? One can talk about illiteracy, ignorance, lack of sanitation and housing — but at the level of three hundred dollars or less per person a year, these are refinements. The most basic fact is that most of them usually go hungry or suffer the irreparable effects of childhood malnutrition. And this in an age when luxury in the rich nations approaches the fantastic.

It is precisely in the countries which produce too little to feed themselves that population is soaring. Before World War II, many of the underdeveloped countries exported grain. Now, most of them import it in ever increasing amounts. Food production in poorer countries has risen by nearly 30 per cent in the period between 1955 and 1965. However, population growth diluted most of this gain so the food gain per person was only 1 per cent. Food production in the industrialized countries meanwhile increased 14 per cent per person. "The gap is rapidly widening between a white, complacent, highly bourgeois, very wealthy, very small North Atlantic elite and everybody else," writes the British economist Barbara

Ward, "and this is not a very comfortable heritage to leave to one's children."

The years 1960-1970 have been designated by the United Nations as "Development Decade." It was hoped that the underdeveloped countries would be able to increase their national income in this decade by 5 per cent a year. Actually, the results so far have been something under 4 per cent. But even if the desired growth rate were achieved, it would take the underdeveloped countries (if present population growth remained constant) from eighty to two hundred years to reach the economic level of Western Europe, and from one hundred and twenty to three hundred years to reach the level of the United States — *as these levels are now.* But of course the economies of Western nations are in fact soaring compared to the tortuously slow growth in the underdeveloped world. At present rates, the underdeveloped world is falling steadily behind.

Obviously the gap between rich and poor nations is not the fault of the rich nations, but a measure of their success. We cannot, however, leave most of the world's people in misery while we race ahead to greater and greater luxury. We cannot do this even if we would like to. For we are living in an age of worldwide revolution — the "revolution of rising expectations" — and America, the symbol of universal wealth and success, cannot escape the revolution's effects.

Everywhere in the underdeveloped world, hundreds of millions of human beings, having recently emerged from foreign domination, are struggling to emerge from the much more powerful domination of hunger, disease,

ignorance — of short, brutish, nasty lives lived on the borderline of survival. The knowledge that destitution and
physical suffering are not the immutable destiny of mankind has released an unparalleled surge of raw aspiration
throughout the world. Dynamic, sometimes explosive,
forces of nationalism and revolution are sweeping Africa,
Asia and Latin America. The pressures of multiplying
wants, the desire for relief — for *quick* relief — are increasing far out of proportion to the ability of the countries involved to provide relief. The conditions of the poor
majority of the world are not significantly less tolerable
than before. But in this age of revolution, these conditions
appear intolerable to those who must endure them — and
all the more so because the prosperous nations glitter before their eyes.

These are the revolutionary drives that move most of
the world's peoples. They are not difficult for Americans
to understand, for the struggle for better living conditions
is in a sense the history of America. But it *is* difficult for
Americans to grasp the scope of the misery, the distance
between actual living conditions and anything remotely
resembling a decent standard, and the frustrations and
bitterness produced by the disparity between desire and
reality. These can be felt only by those who live in the appalling slums and rural shacks of the world's underprivileged areas which lie far from tourist routes.

There are those who believe that all of the problems,
pressures and passions generated in those slums and
shacks are produced by a Communist conspiracy. But that
is absurd. For they would exist, and would confront us,
had Marx, Lenin, Stalin and Mao Tse-tung never lived.
To regard these problems, pressures and passions as the

work of a sinister plot fomented by scheming Communist agents is an illusion. Communists do try to magnify the frustrations of poor peoples and profit from those frustrations. But the frustrations are already there. They are produced by profound economic, technological, social and demographic forces — in short, by the forces which are making most of the people of the poor nations poorer, day by day. More than anything, Western — and especially American — achievements have stimulated these great forces. More than anything, the aspirations of the non-Western world have been whetted by American success.

Yet these fundamental facts are virtually forgotten in our desperate efforts to fight Communism. American foreign policy has been directed almost exclusively to the single goal of "stopping the spread of the Communist conspiracy" — as if the growing gap in living standards between a South American peasant barely able to feed his family and a skilled American worker shopping for his second car would somehow be closed if only Communists would surrender their evil ambitions; as if the misery and aspirations, appeals and resentments of the underdeveloped lands would disappear if only we could "defeat Communism." Again, as in the approach to our major domestic issues, our attention has been directed to the symptoms of this problem, rather than to the causes. Many people — and Republican congressional leaders as well as their Democratic counterparts are prominent among them — who want most fervently to stop Communism also resist most determinedly the only measures that have a hope of eliminating the underlying causes of Communism. They rely instead upon the narrow theory that military power is the sum and substance of foreign policy, and upon the illusory hope that Communism, which is primarily a political movement, can be stopped by arms and alliances.

We are spending immense sums of money and reserves of energy to supply dozens of countries with tanks, guns and military advice — for measures which can provide temporary relief at best — but at the same time, we are largely ignoring the real sources of discontent, the misery of most of the world's population.

We must of course do everything we can to stop the spread of Communism. As the strongest free nation in the world, we must, in our own interest, as well as in theirs, protect other free nations against aggression and subversion, and by military means if necessary. But fighting Communism by military means is not the only effort required. Our primary effort should be to help these countries cope with their enormous social and economic problems, and in so doing, help transform "have-not" peoples to "haves."

Fighting Communism is a negative pursuit; it puts us on the defensive. Only a positive approach — fighting the conditions that spawn Communism — offers promise of permanent results. With rare exceptions, Communism breeds only in poverty, backwardness and despair. Only societies that offer their people real hope for food, clothing, shelter and pleasure — for escaping the misery into which they were born — can be permanently protected against Communism. For if Communism has appeal in underdeveloped lands, it is only because it promises to satisfy certain basic needs of those countries. Only in a society with an economic base strong enough to provide a decent standard of living for its people can individualism, free enterprise, representative government and the spiritual values we cherish hope to flourish.

Since the end of World War II, we have given over one hundred billion dollars in foreign economic and military aid. (This figure seems quite impressive until put in proper perspective. But in fact nearly half of this assistance was used for our massive postwar aid and development programs in Western Europe. These programs were tremendously successful and were invaluable in helping Western Europe make the transition from the ravages of war to the prosperity and growth of peace. But only a relatively small number of people, in global terms, were affected. And the countries had already experienced the indistrial revolution with all the acquired skills that that fact embraces. Over one-third of the foreign aid appropriation which has been used in underdeveloped countries *has* gone into military assistance. Since most of the balance is absorbed in administrative expenses, food shipments and other scattered programs, precious little of our total aid has been available for direct economic assistance to the masses of people in underdeveloped lands.) Toward what end? We cannot hope to purchase the affection and respect of the underdeveloped peoples, as Russia, China and even India in the small aid program it maintains in neighboring Nepal have discovered. And this is true no matter how gracefully we dispense our gifts. The affection of the underdeveloped world is simply not for sale. And though we desire it we do not need it. What we do need, however, is the stability of the underdeveloped world. And what we can hope for is that our aid will make underdeveloped countries independent in fact as well as form — economically self-sufficient as well as politically sovereign. We can hope to give aid in ways which will help establish conditions under which aid will not be needed forever. And we can hope, by helping to provide the opportunity for economic self-development, to lessen the sources of resentment against America and the temptation to resort to Communist alliances and Communist methods.

The primary goal of foreign aid, in other words, must be to help supply that which is most essential for the self-development of underdeveloped countries, and which the countries are least able to supply themselves: investment in long-range, fundamental projects which will make possible further economic progress. We must plan our aid with the overriding goal of introducing technical, agricultural and industrial skills for the great masses of population, and the development of the human and natural resources essential for a productive economy in twentieth-century terms. Not every underdeveloped country can become a major industrial power, with its own steel mills and machine-tool plants. But there is a vast need in all underdeveloped countries to establish the foundation for a productive economy. This means building roads, dams, communications and transportation systems, industrial and fertilizer plants — whatever is best suited to develop the economic potential of individual countries. And it means teaching the skills required to operate these fundamental facilities. Unless this is done, the underdeveloped countries have no hope of becoming self-sufficient. In terms of needs, precious little of our foreign aid is directed to the development of these long-term economic projects. Consider the figures from the point of view of the recipient

[224]

countries. According to United Nations' studies, roughly one-half of all foreign assistance received by underdeveloped countries is exhausted simply in maintaining living standards, and a third is used to repay earlier foreign debts. (American aid used to be given primarily in the form of grants, rather than loans, but many recipient countries felt that outright grants insulted their dignity. Now 70 per cent of United States aid takes the form of low-interest, long-term loans. In spite of extremely generous terms, however, the underdeveloped countries simply cannot meet their repayment obligations and at the same time hope to make economic progress.) The seventy-five "developing" countries must in the coming years pay 4 to 5 billion dollars a year to service their foreign debts. This places a tremendous burden on their resources. Our own economic aid, it should be remembered, is just over 2 billion dollars a year — just half the amount the developing countries must pay for debt servicing. India, for example, will have to use half its current foreign aid for repayment of past debts. Obviously, some kind of resettlement or postponement of these debts is necessary. It is not feasible to return to the system of grants. The United States should take the initiative to secure general recognition of this problem and a worldwide agreement for its solution. Debtor states are reluctant to raise the issue. But associating all creditor and debtor states with an effort to find a solution would emphasize the common interest of all in the fortunes of the poor nations. With one-half of foreign aid being consumed simply to maintain pitifully low living standards, and a third being consumed to repay earlier debts, a mere seventeen per cent is left for productive projects. Again, it is simply not enough.

The example of India serves as a fair illustration of the magnitude of the problem and the insufficiency of the resources available to cope with it. The average Indian peasant now earns nineteen cents a day. The Indian government's most optimistic plans for economic development would add one cent a day to each peasant's income every year — the amount would be twenty cents a day in 1966, twenty-one cents in 1967, and so on. And even this meager improvement is threatened by a lack of resources for development.

These are the facts — grim now, and certain to become more grim in the coming decades. As Ambassador Stevenson said in the last article he wrote before his death, "To assume that the world can continue half-affluent and half-desperate is to assume a patience on the part of the needy for which —to put it mildly — history gives us no warrant at all." Whether we like it or not, the solution, I believe, lies in giving greater aid to underdeveloped countries, and aid specifically directed toward long-term development of industrial and agricultural resources which themselves will produce wealth in the future. Only by giving more aid in the form which is most valuable — to help build "producer" goods which in turn will produce more goods — can we hope to achieve our objectives in these countries.

It would be fortunate if we could limit our foreign aid program to its present size, merely shifting allocations to give greater emphasis to industrial and agricultural-development projects. But I believe this would be a great mistake. Foreign aid is given for a variety of purposes — to relieve human suffering, to help countries maintain their independence and security, to influence countries, as well as to assist in the development of economic resources. Surplus American foodstuffs are desperately needed to alleviate hunger and malnutrition; India, Pakistan and Turkey, for example, would have suffered mass starvation in the past three years without surplus food from the United States. And surplus foodstuffs also help underdeveloped countries save their precious hard currency by obviating the need to buy grain abroad. Loans for general purposes are also essential, to help underdeveloped countries buy raw materials, machinery, and spare parts abroad. To cut down on these programs in favor of others would be to put the underdeveloped countries in even greater distress. What is needed is not merely a shifting of allocations. There is need for an increase in the total amount of American aid. We must continue to ship surplus food and carry on our other programs but we must spend more funds for industrial and agricultural development.

I suggest greater aid in spite of the tendency of many Americans to grow weary of foreign aid programs. For what is our alternative? I think less aid would mean disaster for the United States. And in a sense we *are* giving less and less aid each year: as our gross national product expands, our allocations for foreign economic aid are remaining constant — meaning we are spending a smaller and smaller percentage of our national wealth for one of the most vital of our national interests. While the 2.2 billion dollars we presently spend on foreign economic aid is a considerable sum, we should remember that we Americans are able to spend 13.6 billion dollars annually on liquor and 7.8 billion dollars annually on tobacco.

Increased foreign aid is not to be confused with philanthropy or altruism. Aside from the beneficial side-effects it causes in our own domestic economy (in 1962, for example, our aid programs financed over 20 per cent of American exports of iron and steel, and over 30 per cent of exports of locomotives and chemical fertilizers), it is a matter of pragmatic international politics. How long can we remain secure while the majority of the world's population lives in hunger and despair, and those who wish to undermine our influence stand ready to exploit this dissatisfaction?

And increased foreign aid for development of resources is a matter of pragmatic economics too. We are spending 3 to 4 billion dollars freely this year in South Vietnam to stop the spread of Communism, largely by military means. Yet we are spending only 340 million dollars — reluctantly — this year to assist the economic development of India. Surely it is wiser to spend the billions for constructive economic development in countries which, if prosperous, would become effective counterweights to Communist China, than to spend billions for military operations which by themselves cannot promise any kind of effective counterweights. Surely it is better to increase our investments in foreign assistance now in order to prevent the need for far more vast military expenditures later. Surely it is saner to build now in order to obviate the need to bomb later.

The conduct of American foreign affairs is, in broad outline, bipartisan. However, Republicans can make a particularly rich contribution in the administration of foreign aid. It seems logical that Republicans should be the natural leaders in this area. The Republican tradition — that part of it of which we are proud — lends itself to making hard decisions. Republicans are likely to be expert in understanding the need for capital investment and directing its use. And Republicans are temperamentally attuned to helping people help themselves, which is the central goal of our foreign aid programs.

We have observed that one of the primary needs of our foreign policy is strengthening the economies of the underdeveloped nations toward the goal of self-sufficiency. And who is better equipped than the Republican Party to help plan this economic development? The Democratic approach to the plight of underdeveloped countries, like its approach to our domestic problems, has failed to direct itself primarily to the source of the problems, and therefore has committed us to treating the symptoms indefinitely. Our foreign aid programs *have* helped the underdeveloped lands, but they *have not* been directed primarily to helping people of those lands help themselves. Development of their own industries, their own skills, their own capital, their own agriculture — their own base for rapid economic growth, and with it the ability to guide their own political destiny — offers the only promise of permanent solution.

The men who developed America's industries, invested capital, and directed America's phenomenal economic growth were overwhelmingly Republican; and the men who manage American industry and capital at the highest level are still overwhelmingly Republican. If anyone in the world is equipped to solve the underlying problems of the underdeveloped countries, these men are. The skills are theirs in abundance; it is the interest and will to grapple with the problems that is needed.

Here is another superb opportunity to provide enlightened leadership in foreign affairs anticipating the needs of the coming decades. The present threat to America's security is greater than was the threat of fascism. The problems of the underdeveloped lands are more subtle and the response required of Americans more sophisticated. Painful decisions and prolonged sacrifices are going to be required of America in dealing with the underdeveloped world in the coming decades. There is no way to avoid this. Let us, then, as Republicans take advantage of this opportunity for leadership.

A reasonable, flexible approach to the administration of long-term economic projects under foreign aid is also needed. We must recognize the problems of economic development of the countries involved and approach their solution in terms of local needs and capabilities, not in terms of a mere repetition of past American economic development. We must be flexible and pragmatic, not rigid and dogmatic. Where a new economic project can best be accomplished in the framework of a nationalized industry, we must not retreat from undertaking that project because it is "socialistic." In the nineteenth century, American steel mills, for example, began as small workshops in the garages or backyards of individuals. That of course was private enterprise. It began and grew as a private project. But when an underdeveloped country undertakes to build a steel mill in the twentieth century — a steel mill which, in order to compete efficiently in the world market, requires hundreds of millions of dollars in investment — that enterprise is often a matter of national, public concern. In many underdeveloped countries, huge economic projects which bear upon the economic development of the entire country quite naturally must start as nationalized enterprises. And an unwillingness on our part to recognize this necessity can only hurt our interests abroad and help those of the Communists.

The episode involving the Bokaro steel mill in India is the most glaring example of the consequences of American dogmatism toward "socialistic" enterprises. Indian industrialists pleaded with American officials to help build that steel mill on a nationalized basis because, they affirmed, their own private resources of capital and technological expertise were not equal to the task. In spite of what Indian businessmen themselves said, however, the United States Congress retracted its support of the project on the grounds that it damaged the interests of free enterprise. The result was a double loss of face to the United States: after years of pledges and plans, we rejected the proposal. That was bad enough. But when the Soviet Union happily took over support of the project, our prestige in India and in the underdeveloped world sank still further.

By its nature, foreign aid is essentially a governmental affair. I believe Republican strategy should assume the leadership of its planning and administration. But aside from governmental foreign aid, there is a vast opportunity for Republicans to help develop the underdeveloped countries in a nongovernmental way.

I suggest that the Republican Party propose the establishment of a foreign business corps, whose purpose would be to help develop the private and public industries, businesses and agricultural enterprises of the underdeveloped lands. Nowhere is there a greater pool of industrial and agricultural skills and talents than in the United States.

Nowhere are these skills and talents so desperately needed as in the underdeveloped world. And nowhere is there a more superb opportunity for Republicans to do something creative, constructive, and consistent with our traditions.

We have seen the benefits of the Peace Corps in its four years of operation. Despite certain shortcomings, it has achieved gratifying results with minimal expenditures. But the Peace Corps is composed largely of young people, recently graduated from high school or college. To be sure, their skills and particularly their enthusiasm are put to good use in underdeveloped lands. But the skills and experience of business executives, department heads, engineers and management experts would be far more valuable. These are the people who have the most to offer in the development of private enterprise in underdeveloped lands. Until now their human resources have gone largely untapped because of a lack of leadership in organizing an effective program. That American businessmen are not in the thick of the struggle to develop the businesses of foreign land seems to me the most glaring shortcoming in America's approach to foreign aid.

And this is a shortcoming, despite the existence of the International Executive Service Corps, rudely known as the "Paunch Corps." This corps channels retired American business executives, or mid-career executives who want to broaden their experience, into brief consultative services to business concerns in the newly developing nations. The executives receive no pay, but their expenses and those of their wives are paid for by the foreign businesses and they are not allowed to stay with any one company more than three or four months. This innovation, at least, shows a recognition of the problem. And to the extent that the program exists, it is good.

But much more could and should be done. A comprehensive, well-planned and well-administered foreign business corps should be established. American volunteers would be assigned to one or another enterprise abroad for a period of one or two years as advisors, assistants and consultants. They would be given leaves of absence by their American business firms for the duration of their service abroad without loss of seniority or promotion benefits. Their purpose would be to help native firms develop their own opportunities for growth, efficiency and the development of new products and techniques. They would be lending their skills in the most direct, rational way, the way which offers the greatest promise of immediate and long-range benefits to the economies of underdeveloped lands.

A foreign business corps composed of American business personnel in the prime of their business life could, I think, make a vast contribution to closing the gap between the rich and poor nations. The problems of economic development in underdeveloped lands are staggering, and the American contribution to their solution is restricted by nature. But in terms of what could be done, a business corps would, I think, help achieve maximum results.

The business corps would encounter problems, of course. The most important would be whether businessmen of underdeveloped countries would in fact be eager to receive Americans as advisers. It goes without saying that no program would be feasible without the permission, indeed the request, of the recipient countries. But talking with foreign businessmen and government officials and with American professors versed in the affairs of underdeveloped lands has convinced me that most underdeveloped countries would in fact eagerly welcome American businessmen. Once it is made clear that the purpose of the business corps is the development of native private enterprises for their own growth and profit, I believe the concept would have tremendous appeal in most underdeveloped lands. In those lands where it has no appeal, of course, we will have to limit ourselves to the traditional methods of foreign aid.

A second problem would be finding active American businessmen willing to interrupt their careers for a year or two to devote to this undertaking. I would not expect tens of thousands of volunteers to appear in the program's first year. But I do feel that a small percentage of businessmen are eager to make a contribution in the way that they can best make it — and a small percentage of businessmen, even one per cent, would be quite enough. From a modest beginning, the program might grow into a truly major undertaking. The businessmen would suffer no loss in their salaries, which would be paid by the federal government. Besides this, the personal rewards would also be great in many cases. I genuinely believe that for many American businessmen the year or two spent in this challenging and stimulating cause would be one of the most satisfying and productive periods of their lives. Americans have a strong strain of idealism and an eagerness to serve a great cause. Here is a way for businessmen to exercise their idealism in the most fruitful way.

A third problem would be finding businessmen flexible enough to withstand the cultural shock of working in underdeveloped lands, and flexible enough to adapt themselves to local conditions, customs and levels of business knowledge. They unquestionably would find vast differences in the problems faced by local businesses, the personnel skills available, and even the willingness to work well! Here the problem may be more serious than in the case of Peace Corps volunteers who, being for the most part young, are by nature adaptable to change. But many American businessmen also have proved themselves superbly adaptable to change. When it was necessary during the war, American businessmen in military uniforms built landing strips, ports, roads and dams under the most trying circumstances imaginable. In operating their own firms, they have often overcome great barriers in working in foreign lands. The initial disorientation caused by cultural differences and differences in business techniques may indeed startle business corps volunteers. But in time they will adapt themselves to local conditions and they will be invaluable in helping local business adapt to the conditions necessary for efficient enterprise in the twentieth century. The exposure of business groups and volunteers to actual working conditions in foreign lands will help build in America a precious source of understanding of foreign policy. Having returned home after their year or two of service, the business corps volunteers will provide a new source of information which will help in the formation of an enlightened, creative American foreign policy.

A foreign business corps would face many difficulties, but none I can envisage would be insuperable. Careful planning would be required to work out the details of the program — but now it is the approach, initiative, the leadership that is most wanted. It may be discovered in time that vice presidents of firms are less valuable as advisers to businesses abroad than engineers and managers at a lower working level where the problems of American and native businesses are more likely to have common elements. It will be, of course, essential to supply the right people at the right level for the right businesses in the right countries. But even where engineers and foremen and factory and agricultural technicians are the people to be sent abroad, American businessmen will nevertheless be involved at the highest level. For their absence from their firms will, hopefully, be approved and supported as a matter of their firms' general policy. And indeed the whole concept of a nationwide dynamic foreign business corps would have no hope of success unless it were planned and administered by American business at the highest level.

I suggest that we draw American businessmen more closely into the struggle to close the gap between the rich and poor nations, not only because it is morally right that they do this and because they will get great satisfaction out of discharging their moral obligation, but also because they are in fact the people best qualified to achieve results.

Mr. Sol Linowitz, Xerox Corporation board chairman, has correctly said, "The best way to exchange knowledge is to wrap it up in a person." And the knowledge that the underdeveloped countries so desperately need is found largely in American businessmen.

The establishment of a foreign business corps coupled with investment by American business on a far more geographically diversified basis than at present would reap political and economic benefit both for the United States and for the underdeveloped nations of the world.

Presently the bulk of American private business investment abroad is concentrated in Western Europe. And while American business investment totals many millions of dollars, there has been relatively no anti-American political backlash in Western European countries. In those countries American investments are diversified and cover almost the entire range of the industrial spectrum. The American businessmen who have had the foresight to make the investments have realized a handsome profit, but the Western European nations into which the investments have been funneled have shared the dividends, for almost without exception the investments have bolstered the economy of the Western European nations.

But it is important to make a distinction between the political and economic stability of the Western European nations and the countries in the Middle East and Latin America where there has also been investment by American businessmen. Whereas political stability is the common characteristic of most Western European countries, the opposite tends to be true in Latin America and the Middle East, where stable government like a stable economy has traditionally been difficult to maintain. In Latin America and the Middle East, this political and economic problem has been compounded by the fact that the overwhelming bulk of American investment in that part of the world has been in mining, petroleum producing, and smelting — in *extracting* natural resources rather than, as has been the case in Western Europe, *developing* indigenous industries. The extraction of natural resources by foreign capital has been both politically and economically unhealthy for Latin American and Middle Eastern countries, where in most cases there is economic dependence

[237]

upon the extraction of a single natural resource. When the terms of trade become unfavorable for the supplier of these raw materials or, as inevitably happens, the raw material itself is "mined out" the country faces disaster. For once the resource is exhausted, nothing of permanent value is left in the underdeveloped countries, since most of the extracted raw materials are shipped to America and Western Europe for manufacture. We have seen, in our own country, the social and economic tragedy which has sometimes occurred in a city or town which becomes dependent upon one company, one industry, or one mineral. The stakes are obviously much greater and the political consequences far more dangerous when a *nation's* economic survival depends upon a single natural resource.

Investment in extracting natural resources does not promote political stability and does very little to develop the industrial potential of an underdeveloped country. However, since royalties are paid for the raw materials extracted, some temporary economic benefit does accrue. But the royalties do not provide the permanent benefits which would result from investment in agricultural and industrial production.

There is not necessarily an inherent conflict between the goals of American private investment abroad and the goals of our nation's foreign policy — but neither is there, necessarily, a community of interest.

Poverty and famine abroad could once be ignored by the wealthy nations of the world. But perhaps the most important lesson that the United States has learned in the last generation is that poverty and famine are the handmaidens of world political instability. Millions of men and women in every corner of the globe now aspire to the economic security and stability — the individual dignity — the political independence which the United States and most of the countries in Western Europe enjoy. To ignore those aspirations would be dangerous.

Where American investments are so vast that the economies of underdeveloped countries and their governments are largely controlled by American firms, there are understandable reasons for resentment. And where American business investments serve, by intention or otherwise, to help protect the status quo in those countries (one or two per cent of the population owning the vast bulk of land and wealth) despite the desperate need for social and economic change, our investments are damaging American political interests.

Increasing discontent and increasing anti-Americanism can only lead to revolution followed by the establishment of new governments hostile to the United States. The experience of Cuba is too recent to be forgotten. If revolutionary governments feel that American capital controls their major industries so that they cannot plan their own economies and develop their own resources, American investments will be expropriated. And there is a danger that the governments will align themselves in one form or another with Communism.

American businessmen who wish to invest in the underdeveloped nations of Latin America and the Middle East must understand that the political realities of the last half of the twentieth century are just as important as a profit-and-loss statement. And the United States government should encourage American businessmen to diversify their private investments in these sections of the world. We must give more in the way of American expertise in helping these nations to build their own economies. American business — for selfish as well as altruistic reasons — must become the partner of underdeveloped nations in building a sound economy based on multiple rather than on single industries or products.

By itself, foreign capital is not harmful to underdeveloped countries. On the contrary, it is absolutely essential to their development. These countries desperately need capital, and Western nations — now America more than any other — need their natural resources. The exchange can be mutually beneficial. Nations *ought* to help one another with what they can supply best. But we must remember that others have national pride. Others want the kind of economic independence which the United States has so long enjoyed. If American business and industry in partnership with our government and the governments and peoples of the underdeveloped countries of Latin America and the Middle East pursued a policy of enlightened self-interest — of mutual give-and-take — many of our present foreign policy problems would be resolved to the satisfaction of all.

To a very great extent, American business has practically ignored Africa insofar as investment is concerned and has been extremely selective in its investments in Asia. In addition to providing economic assistance and in addition to the foreign business corps suggested, the American government should encourage American business to invest in Africa and Asia. Special incentives should be provided for American businessmen who are willing to invest in capital industries on those continents. The economic "shot in the arm" which such investments would bring to the underdeveloped nations in Africa and Asia is incalculable. This kind of a three-pronged offensive which would truly be helping people to help themselves would go a long way toward making those new nations economically stable and politically independent. Such a policy — such a constructive partnership by the American government, American businessmen and the people and governments of those underdeveloped countries would certainly have more value than merely increasing our relief shipments of surplus food and supplies abroad. "Give a man a fish and he will eat well that day," says the Chinese proverb. "Teach him to fish and he will eat for the rest of his days."

Developing the underdeveloped countries and closing the gap between their destitution and our luxury is a task of staggering proportions. It is not so simple a matter as teaching people how to fish. America's role is by nature limited: even with our great wealth and technological knowledge, we could not develop underdeveloped countries within one or two decades even if they were ours to develop — which, obviously, they are not. No single course of action promises a magic solution. Nevertheless, America must make what efforts it can (and it can make very much greater efforts than it is now making) to help solve the underlying problems of the world's underdeveloped lands. For unless the problems are solved, the world will become increasingly tense, antagonistic and explosive for our generation and, even more, for our children and their children's generation.

The World Food and Agriculture Organization estimates that ten thousand people a day now die from the direct and indirect effects of hunger. Two billion people — two-thirds of the world's population — are underfed.

[241]

And the world's population will *double* in the next thirty-five years. The grave problems of the great masses of underdeveloped peoples are almost certain to worsen before they improve.

The great questions are, will they improve at all, and is America willing to commit herself to an intense, genuine effort to make them improve? I believe the answer to both questions is yes. I further believe that the Republican Party will draw upon its tradition of facing hard facts and unpleasant problems, and upon its great skills, to lead America in a determined attack upon the basic causes of world tension.

TWENTY

✤ ✤ ✤

A Conservative Philosophy

THROUGHOUT this book I have made frequent and favorable references to Abraham Lincoln and Theodore
Roosevelt. I have quoted them extensively with particular
reference to their philosophy relating to the power and
responsibility of the federal government. And from the
quotations cited, the reader might well conclude that
both Lincoln and Roosevelt were liberals in every sense of
the word. But in fact both Lincoln and Roosevelt were
true conservatives. Lincoln treasured the past. He was instinctively conservative. He used the powers of government creatively because he sensed that lack of government action often leads to the destruction of traditional
ideals and customs, not to their conservation. Theodore
Roosevelt, too, beneath his zeal was by nature deeply conservative. With his imaginative, forceful leadership, he
managed to conserve those aspects and qualities of rural
nineteenth-century America which were suited to the urban twentieth century. "Both his preferences and aver-
sions were so orthodox," George Mayer has written, "that
Roosevelt became a symbol of older America slowly van-
ishing in the wake of the new industrial society . . .

[243]

Roosevelt's every act seemed to say: We can preserve our national character irrespective of the challenges delivered by the Twentieth Century."

And let it not go unchallenged that conservatism has no political appeal in mid-twentieth-century America. The American character is complex and contradictory; in many aspects it is oriented toward the future, not the past. Yet one of its strongest strains is an instinctive, persistent conservatism, which responds immediately to authentic conservative leadership. Perhaps President William Howard Taft was overenthusiastic when he called America "the most conservative country in the world." But Professor Rossiter, a prominent scholar of American conservatism, can hardly be accused of partisanship. "For all our self-congratulatory talk of innovation and progress," he has written, "we are a most conservative people."

A profound respect for stability and respectability, for orderly and traditional patterns of government lies near the center of the American political soul. The Republican Party should be able to turn that respect to good account. Senator Goldwater has said repeatedly that of the two major parties, ours logically must represent conservative sentiment in America. I agree. But what is conservatism? How ought it to be interpreted and applied? Here is where we have gone astray. Not conservatism is responsible for the Republican decline, but a severe distortion of conservatism which has robbed it of its potentially great appeal.

"A state without the means of some change is without the means of its conservation," wrote Edmund Burke, the prince of Anglo-American conservatism. Yet in this decade, conservatism in America has been made to appear as blind, intractable opposition to all change — or, more specifically, opposition to all attempts by government to cope with change. It is represented as a determination for government to do little or nothing. Or worse: a determination to dismantle many great achievements of the past. To Negroes, conservatism has come to mean opposition to civil rights; to elderly people, opposition to social security; to poor farmers, opposition to rural electrification; to the people of the Tennessee Valley, opposition to the T.V.A. To the great majority of American voters, conservatism has lost all appeal because it seems to be telling them that social security, civil rights, Medicare, urban renewal, rural electrification — measures and institutions that they consider essential to their well-being — are sinful or un-American. Conservatism has come to mean: "Stop! Thou shall progress no further. What you cannot do for yourselves does not deserve to be done." This is a perversion of authentic conservatism and an invitation to electoral defeat.

Genuine conservatism in the Republican Party has been shunted aside by a jumble of oversimplified, misleading articles of faith which trade wishful thinking for economic and social reality, and appeals to ancient virtues for rational planning about what to do next. There has always been a danger of misrepresenting conservatism in this way, but Senator Goldwater has, alas, made the danger a clear and present reality.

"The Conservative approach," wrote the Senator in his provocative *Conscience of a Conservative*, "is nothing more or less than an attempt to apply the wisdom and experience and the revealed truths of the past to the problems of today. The challenge is not to find new truths, but

The Challenge of Change

to learn how to apply established truths to the problems of today." True enough — but what are the "wisdom" and "experience," the "revealed" and "established" truths of the past? In politics, I have found few "revealed" truths besides the truisms that problems must be solved, forces balanced, and needs met as they are in most other aspects of life. Of course they must be solved legally and constitutionally; that is why we preserve the Constitution and the Supreme Court. (Senator Goldwater's incessant references to the Constitution and our supposed violations of it are unconvincing. If in fact we are subverting the Constitution, why do the best legal minds of the nation fail to recognize the subversion?) Of course we must take into consideration all that has gone before; a politician who fails to do that stands little chance of being elected, and less of being reelected. But it is ludicrous to believe that we can find the solutions to problems of, say, unemployment caused by automation simply by searching for the revealed truths of the past. Burke, again, destroys this illusion. "What is the use of discussing a man's abstract right to food or medicine?" he wrote. "The question is upon the method of procuring and administering them. In that deliberation, I shall always advise to call in the aid of the farmer and the physician, rather than the professor of metaphysics."

One of Senator Goldwater's favorite themes invokes the "ancient and tested truths" which "lie at the heart of the American political system." "The ancient and tested truths which guided our Republic through its earlier days," he wrote, "will do equally well for us." The implication here, of course — as in the Senator's constant refer-

[246]

ences to "our forefathers," "the Founding Fathers," and "our sacred political heritage" — is that the first generation of Americans established something universal and immutable; that by "tampering" with their work we are despoiling the American political heritage and robbing ourselves and future generations of their birthright as Americans; and that the overriding duty of conservatism is to fight to prevent all change. By oversimplification and distortion this interpretation of conservatism makes it a dead doctrine, irrational and unworkable.

First, it should be pointed out that not ancient or tested truths guided our Republic through its early days, but new — and in those days, radical — propositions. That men were born free and created equal, that human rights are inviolable, that government was established in order to insure all citizens Life, Liberty and the Pursuit of Happiness — these were brilliant new theories, consciously instituted as the foundation of government for the first time in history. The United States was a new nation offering new hope based on new theories of man, society and government. The very word "republic" was synonymous with "radicalism" in that age of monarchies. No doubt "conservatives" of Senator Goldwater's leaning would have denounced constitutional republicanism in those days as wildly irresponsible.

Most of the Founding Fathers were men of property and conservative by temperament. Yet in the work of establishing the Republic's new political institutions, they were nothing if not innovators. All that the Founding Fathers created — the Constitution, Federalism, the Supreme Court, the Bill of Rights, the separation of legislative, executive and judicial powers — was either totally original, or originally applied to the workings of a national government. The conventional slogans about the Founding Fathers suggest that it was their will to change nothing but to make the old order permanent. In fact, their experience suggests precisely the opposite.

It is perfectly true, however, that many of the "truths" arrived at during the early days of the Republic *will* do equally well for us. The question is, which truths? What should we take from our progenitors, use to solve our problems, and pass to our progeny? *What do we want to conserve?* Obviously not a set of legislative truths. If the legislative work of the early days of the Republic would do equally well for us, we would now be crippled with laws regulating the use of slaves, horses and craft guilds — and unable to deal with automobiles, railroads, wonder drugs, and everything else which has been introduced into American life since the eighteenth century. If the Founding Fathers thought they could solve the problems of succeeding ages, they would have simply enacted a set of permanent laws, and dispensed with legislatures of the future. A Republic of this sort would not have endured a year.

But this is absurd. No rational system of government has ever pretended to eliminate change. What the Founding Fathers really established was the opposite: a rational, pragmatic and eminently workable system for *effecting* change. For the Constitution, and the political machinery it created, is more than anything an instrument for coping with change. It has given the United States a political stability enjoyed by few nations. But as Metternich, still another great conservative statesman, has observed, "governments, in establishing the principle of stability will in no wise exclude the development of what is good, for stability is not immobility."

That the Constitution has worked splendidly to accommodate the tempestuous changes of the past one hundred and fifty-odd restless years speaks eloquently of the magnificent ingenuity and acumen of the Founding Fathers. But not only of the Founding Fathers. Had there not followed generations of Americans in the Supreme Court and elsewhere who were masters of the political arts of compromise and accommodation to change, the Constitution would have long been scrapped. And precisely this is what must be conserved of the American political heritage: the Constitutional machinery and the spirit of compromise — the tools for dealing with change.

The notion that the Constitution somehow forbids us to launch new programs to cope with social and economic problems is pernicious nonsense. This is just what the Founding Fathers did *not* want the Constitution to be. The very essence of their design for government — now "ancient and tested" — is a set of rules, procedures, and restrictions according to which we discuss, debate, propose, approve and repeal social and economic legislation. The Founding Fathers were anything but rigid theorists who denied the need for creative legislation. They were progressive and flexible, and it is futile to invoke their name in defense of standing still. A conservatism based on a simplistic emotional appeal to the heritage of the Founding Fathers does credit neither to the heritage, the Founding Fathers nor the Republican Party.

The *Wall Street Journal,* that pillar of enlightened moderation, attempted to define conservatism some ten years ago. "Conservatism," it said, "is not a policy; nor is it a

The Challenge of Change

program to solve economic or political problems. It is hardly more than an instinctive belief that today's society is built on several thousand years and that in those years men have found things they should fasten to. Out of this grows not opposition to change in political institutions or in economic methods but an awareness that in too hasty flight from the old we can flee to evils we know not of."

It was an admirable attempt to define a concept which really — in spite of Senator Goldwater's generalities — defies definition. Conservatism is indeed a mood or an instinctive belief that the work of past generations should not be discarded without careful thought. But something quite different has been passing for conservatism in America. That something tries to do precisely what genuine conservatism cannot. It tries to substitute as a policy for coping with specific economic and political problems a justification for opposing changes in political institutions and economic methods. As the *Wall Street Journal* warned, this is disastrous. It destroys the delicate balance between stability and flexibility, permanence and change — and destroys the appeal of genuine conservatism.

"For too long," Robert Donovan has written, "the Republicans equated true conservatism with business conservatism, as if there were no conservative philosophy other than that enunciated by the National Association of Manufacturers." No doubt this statement seems slanderous to many Republicans convinced they are defending the conservative cause. But is it entirely without merit? Millions of American voters *do* interpret Republican conservatism as no more or less than business conservatism. They observe that very often what passes for political con-

[250]

servatism happens to coincide precisely with what is desired by business. They notice that "conservatives" very often oppose those programs against which major industries have lobbied mightily. They recognize that "conservative" contentions very often turn out to be repetitions of the contentions of powerful pressure groups — which are primarily concerned with the financial interests of their own members, however much they couch their arguments in terms of the national interest. And most voters do not believe that the similarity between business conservatism and Republican conservatism is mere coincidence. The reliance of political conservatism upon economic conservatism makes political conservatism suspect.

How often do we see "conservatives" of this kind support any measure, propose any plan, offer any idea that might run contrary to the financial interests of big business and the professional class? The interests of big business and the professional class should be represented of course, as should the interests of all people. But to call this conservatism is to reduce an ancient, honored and universal political sentiment to pressure-group tactics. This is not conservatism, but favoritism.

In spite of the efforts of an enlightened business minority, the business community has not generally provided the perceptive foresight and broad perspective essential for national leadership. It has — quite legitimately — provided effective leadership for its own interests. But political leadership cannot rest on so narrow a base. The early American conservatives — Washington, Hamilton, Adams and others — recognized that the needs of national welfare had to supersede the needs of immediate class interests. But some of that sense of responsibility, social obligation, national purpose — of noblesse oblige — has been lost in contemporary Republicanism. It has been sacrificed in favor of protecting short-run business advantage. Conservatism which, intentionally or otherwise, is principally devoted to protecting vested financial and business interests and traditions faces a grim future. There are just too many other interests and traditions to be protected in America. More than sixty years ago, Winston Churchill warned of the barrenness of this kind of conservatism. The "Republican Party in the United States of America," he said, was "rigid, materialistic and secular"; its opinions "turned on tariffs" and it caused the "lobbies to be crowded with the touts of protected industries."

Conservatism must be founded on deep respect and interests in individual men — in their freedom, their security, their opportunity for development, their overall wellbeing. It is absurd to believe that conservatives by definition are uninterested in such problems as water pollution or medical care for the aged or the fate of America's underprivileged minorities. It is nonsensical to assume that conservations must by nature oppose all poverty programs, medical programs, educational programs. Unfortunately, most Americans still make these assumptions. And, unfortunately, conservatism has come to be associated with the protection of institutions, especially of management and industry — not the protection of men.

American conservatism, in short, has been distorted into a rigid, sometimes reactionary denial of duty of government to accommodate to change. But this is less the fault of Senator Goldwater and his followers than those of us who, by our timidity and ineffectuality, have allowed the genuine conservative tradition to be shunted aside. Whether one likes or dislikes Senator Goldwater's interpretation of conservatism, he has defended it forcefully. The spokesmen for traditional conservatism, by contrast, have put our case feebly and defensively. It is time to reassert the principles of enlightened conservatism which alone offer hope of success for the Republican Party in twentieth-century American politics.

Genuine conservatives want to profit from the past, not live in it. They are skeptical about reforms, but willing to accept them — indeed, to propose and engineer them — when they are required. They treasure the past not as a Utopia, but for its insights into the problems of the present and the future. They understand that new problems require new thought and new solutions, and that few problems of a complex, industrialized society can be simply and easily solved. They appreciate that social progress is essential to a society's stability, and that unless changes are made in the superstructure of society, the pressures for change will undermine the foundation of that society. They look forward to the future as a time of opportunity, not a time of trouble.

These were the qualities of Abraham Lincoln and Theodore Roosevelt. And these were also the qualities of "Mr. Conservative," Senator Robert A. Taft. Senator Taft never ceased to *think* about the issues of his day and he never ceased to *learn*. He was proud of his authorship of the Taft-Hartley Act. Yet in 1949, when a bill to repeal "Taft-Hartley" was being debated on the floor of the Senate, Senator Taft candidly told Senator Paul A. Douglas of

[253]

Illinois, "I'm beginning to discover the Taft-Hartley law was an experiment and there are many features which no doubt can be improved in the law."

Senator Taft also had second thoughts about federal aid to education. "I led the fight against the New Deal education bill in 1943, and we beat it. But I had to give the problem a lot of study and saw there was a real need. So I went to [Senator] Lister Hill [Democrat, of Alabama] and the National Education Association, and we worked out a new draft that we all agreed on."

Abraham Lincoln, Theodore Roosevelt, Senator Robert Taft and other distinguished Republican statesmen were instinctively and intellectually conservative — indeed, they were the prototypes of reasoned, responsible men grounded in reality and the American traditions. Their approach to government was positive, as was Burke's — ("government is a contrivance of human wisdom to provide for human wants") — not negative, as is Senator Goldwater's ("throughout history, government has proved to be the chief instrument for thwarting man's liberty"). Genuine conservatism offers the best framework for solving America's problems. Pseudo-conservatism, dedicated to standing still or sliding backward, offers little besides the prospect of letting the problems persist and intensify.

If there is a single quality that separates genuine conservatism from its distorted version, that quality is leadership. Genuine conservatives want to manage, to govern, to *lead.* Having recognized that a problem must be attacked — that its time for solution has arrived — they commit themselves to solving it with concern for sound management, efficient organization, and respect for the individual and the past. Pseudo-conservatives, on the other hand, in

[254]

denying the obligation of government to cope with a problem also deny themselves the opportunity to direct its solution. Conservatism without leadership is meaningless. An approach to government incompatible with leadership is an anomaly. Senator Goldwater's "conservatism" sacrifices the opportunity to guide the nation through periods of change. It leaves the nature of the changes to be determined by drift or by Democratic leadership — and therefore, in the long run, leaves us less to conserve.

The Republican statesmen to whom I have referred as genuine conservatives did not seek reform for reform's sake. On the contrary, by birth and breeding they had an instinctive suspicion of political reform and innovation. They had a vested interest in keeping things as they were. But when reform became necessary, they chose to direct it themselves — at the very least in order to conserve as much as possible of the status quo. Benjamin Disraeli, the great nineteenth-century English statesman who revitalized his then moribund Conservative Party, expressed this thought as clearly as anyone. "In a progressive country," he wrote, "change is constant; and the great question is not whether you should resist change which is inevitable but whether that change should be carried out in deference to the manners, the customs, the laws, the traditions of the people or in deference to abstract principle and arbitrary and general doctrines."

Here, I believe, is where the enlightened conservatism has great potential for leadership. The task is not to oppose change but to help accomplish it in keeping with conservative traditions — to direct it as *we* believe it should be directed. To take creative action in the areas I have mentioned and others with integrity and professional skills, to eliminate waste, to conserve human and material resources, to infuse governmental activities with efficiency and excellence — these are the challenges to conservative leadership. For if we are reluctant to propose and engineer our own solutions to national problems, how will our business, professional and political skills be used? Unless conservatives themselves plan essential reforms, the people best equipped to execute changes will remain uninvolved.

The experience of every Western nation including our own demonstrates that when conservatives do meet the challenge of change, their reforms are invariably more sound and effective than their opponents' alternatives. From the English Reform Bill of 1867 to our own Federal Manpower Development and Training Act of 1962, there is a long history of excellent conservative-sponsored legislation which has deftly blended past traditions with present needs through the use of rational, practical methods.

I have been mentioning English conservatives because I think we have much to learn from them. With all its differences, the English political system resembles the American more than does any other. England and America both basically have a two-party system; both have similar notions of justice and freedom. Yet the English Tory Party — which in social composition, tradition and historical influences is far more authentically conservative than our own Republican Party — has managed to flourish while we have been floundering. Of the twenty years since the end of World War II, the Tory Party has been in power for thirteen, and in 1965 they were but eleven votes shy of the Labor majority. And the Tory Party has accomplished this in spite of changes in Great Britain's economic structure which have been much more far-reaching than the changes of the New Deal.

The secret of the success of English conservatism is its willingness to adapt to, even to propose, necessary social and economic changes. It does not try to preserve every aspect of old England in tact, but accommodates itself to and guides the inevitable changes in order to make them as sensible as possible and to conserve what is most important to conserve: the political traditions and the domestic peace and well-being of the nation. It does not sacrifice its desire to be the governing party to obsolete, unworkable economic dogma. It understands that a government which fails to take positive, creative action to accommodate new social forces is least able to contribute anything to conservatism. The Tory Party has discovered in the course of several centuries that inspiring talk about conservative principles is not enough. For if conservatives do not *act* to make conservatism viable, no one will.

This is the spirit of my proposals for Republican approaches to our major national problems. We all want to preserve the free-enterprise system, the ideal of equal opportunity and the tradition of individual effort which are fundamental to the American experience. We want to preserve domestic and foreign peace and protect the country against class bitterness. We want to preserve the democratic tradition. We want to see it expand — for it must be expanded — in ways compatible to how we have expanded it in the past.

But these goals will not be achieved by themselves. They must be implemented by government action. And they must be implemented before the social and economic forces confronting the nation overwhelm us and leave little to be conserved. "Let us," said Burke, "make the revolution a parent of settlement, not a nursery of future revolutions." Let us now try to make permanent solutions instead of prolonging a revolutionary atmosphere. Let us engineer changes in the superstructure of our society in order to prevent serious damage to its foundations.

This, I believe, is the duty of conservatism.

✤ ✤ ✤

The Challenge of Change

THE Republican Party cannot reverse its decline by thinking of its own needs. It must think primarily of the needs of the country. As Governor Nelson Rockefeller has said, "The Republican Party stands today at the cross-roads of its destiny — its destiny is to save the nation by first saving itself." For political parties are not ends in themselves. They are meant to be agencies for promoting the national welfare, for expressing and shaping the general will.

Yet in a real sense, the fate of the Republican Party itself has become a national issue of major proportions. Ordinarily the interests of the nation far outweigh the interests of any of its political parties. But under present circumstances, the nation has no greater interest than the rebirth of a dynamic Republican Party.

This proposition is illustrated by one of my favorite political stories. It took place in 1933 when Republican fortunes and prospects seemed even more gloomy than they do now. After President Franklin Roosevelt's extraordinary congressional successes during the period known as the Hundred Days — a period in which Republicans all

[259]

but ceased to function as a party — the President asked the late Felix Frankfurter, on the eve of Mr. Frankfurter's trip abroad, for some parting advice. "Get yourself an opposition," Mr. Frankfurter replied.

Get yourself an opposition — it was sage advice, for the country more than for President Roosevelt. No doubt President Lyndon Johnson would not agree that he or the country now need a stronger Republican Party. But in this respect at least, President Johnson is outside the American consensus. For the very foundation of American politics, the two-party system, has been undermined by present Republican weakness. And even the most partisan Democrat agrees that America suffers in every respect when it lacks a strong two-party system.

The two-party system was not established by the Constitution or even by law, but it has become so integral to the workings of American government that any serious damage to it is by the nature of things damage to our entire political structure. We do not now enjoy the benefits of genuine two-party competition. And unless Republican strength is restored, there is no guarantee that we will enjoy those benefits in the foreseeable future.

Do I exaggerate? I fear not. Republican representation in the federal government and in many states is now too meager even to sustain an effective and responsible opposition. It is not so much one-party rule in the totalitarian sense that we must fear, as the breakdown of the checks and balances — the principal advantages — of competition. Our government, like our trials at common law, is grounded in the adversary system. Just as a fair trial in the common law presupposes conflict between two sides roughly equal in skill and resources, good government presupposes conflict between two political parties roughly equal in numbers and influence. When one side is palpably weaker than the other, the system loses its balance, its logic, and soon thereafter, its integrity and effectiveness.

More than fifteen years ago, when Republican fortunes were considerably brighter than they are now, an ardent Democrat, Arthur Schlesinger, Jr., warned that "while Democrats may gain short-run benefits from the present absence of competition, thoughtful members of that party understand the long-run dangers from absence of competition. An essential function of a party in our system is to secure the concurrence of that part of the community which it represents, and if a party becomes so feeble and confused that it turns into an object of public pity or contempt, it can no longer assist in securing that concurrence. As a result, our whole political fabric suffers."

It suffers in a dozen ways. At the local level, the absence of competition encourages wrongdoing by public officials. I have had to spend too much of my time as Attorney General of Massachusetts fighting corruption of elective and appointive officials at state, county and local levels. While I cannot say that one-party government is the sole cause of corruption, my experience has consistently confirmed what is commonly assumed about corruption in government: one-party government provides a climate in which all forms of dishonesty and unethical behavior flourish in the conduct of the public business. I am often chided by people who say I enjoy prosecuting wrongdoers because I am "only getting rid of the Democrats." My answer has been, "There is no one here but Democrats." Actually, I have had to prosecute Republicans and Democrats — but more Democrats, logically enough, because Massachusetts is fast becoming a one-party, Democratic state.

Neither political party has a monopoly on corruption or a monopoly on virtue. But voters *are* creating a Democratic monopoly of public office in Massachusetts and in the nation. A climate therefore exists in which the tendency toward virtue struggles unevenly against the tendency toward corruption.

But the effects of corruption under one-party government cannot be measured simply in terms of stolen dollars, of bought jobs, of conflict of interest. In a larger sense, our very political atmosphere is corrupted by the absence of serious competition. In state capitals and in Washington as well, the conflict of political principles is reduced to a sham battle. Meaningful debate becomes rhetoric for the record. Controversial proposals and decisions lose their sense of controversy. Legislative and administrative policies are no longer hammered out and put to the test of a strong, self-confident opposition, but are handed out, untested, by an overconfident majority party. Effective investigations, careful review in committees, minority reports on legislative proposals, the sharpening and dramatizing of issues in floor debates — these crucial functions are feebly discharged by a feeble minority. The opposition itself, recognizing its impotence, loses its sense of responsibility. And inevitably, the members of a party enjoying a lopsided majority become arrogant and lazy. A system theoretically based on competition between near-equal partners becomes a caricature of that system.

If I were starting in politics today, without question I would join the Republican Party. For here is where the great challenges and opportunities lie. If one wants to participate in the political process and is serious about improving America, here is the opportunity to channel political energy where it will do the most good. Equal work will produce far more results in the Republican Party than in the Democratic Party.

I honestly believe that as the Republican Party goes, so goes the nation. The restoration of the two-party system is but one of many national objectives directly dependent upon the rebirth of a strong, self-confident Republican Party. Beyond this, America's future will be determined largely by the Republican future. If the country continues to be led by an overwhelmingly victorious and complacent Democratic Party which is traditionally oriented to temporary solutions and relief, we will continue to make only agonizingly slow progress toward solving our great underlying problems and encouraging excellence in our national life. We will limp along, hesitant, temporizing, protesting and poorly led.

For the restoration of two-party government in America, I make a plea for active support to intellectuals, to members of minorities, to young voters and to those who have, through family ties and background, through labor-union affiliation, through habit and emphathy, always considered themselves Democrats.

The Republican Party must attract intellectual talent and youthful energy. The Republican Party must broaden its overall base. The Republican Party must not accept the outmoded proposition that the Democratic Party is the logical and natural political home of first-, second-, and third-generation Americans. The Republican Party must, by person-to-person contact, work with people who live in America's cities and demonstrate to them a genuine and sincere concern for their problems and aspirations. This is the only road to Republican recovery. It will be long and the obstacles formidable, but that is all the more reason for intellectuals, minorities, and young people to join the march.

I am well aware that the present leadership of many Republican organizations may not encourage intellectuals, minorities and eager young people to join the Republican Party. But that should not dissuade them, for American intellectuals have always loved challenge and here is an opportunity for them to respond with meaningful political activity to a clear-cut challenge vital to the nation's stability. Here is a chance for them to channel their zeal for improving the country into direct action. It has been all too easy for the nation's intellectuals to stand aside and criticize the Republican Party without committing themselves to its improvement. But those intellectuals who have refused to make the commitment, who have reserved their skills and energy for deriding our condition are no less responsible for that condition than the Republican Party they criticize. To allow the Republican Party to "stew in its own juice" is as irresponsible as some of the positions Republican leaders have taken in the last thirty-five years, and for which intellectuals have most criticized our party.

The same reasons that have disaffected the intellectuals have caused young people to avoid the Republican Party. Since the advent of Franklin D. Roosevelt, members of minority groups have, rightly or wrongly, believed that the Democratic Party would best serve their interests. And immigrants, their children and grandchildren have, by and large, shared that belief. Because of this, the composition of the Republican Party has lacked that pluralistic quality which has benefited the Democratic Party so much. The voices of these groups have not been heard in Republican Party Councils. We learn about their problems secondhand. We have not had the advantages of their thinking or their suggestions for solutions to their problems. Worse, their absence has left an intraparty political void — they have not been present as participants to influence the direction in which the Republican Party should move.

They have maximized their philosophical differences with the Republican Party and minimized their philosophical differences with the Democratic Party. They have put practically all of their political eggs in the Democratic Party basket to the detriment of the two-party system and to their own detriment, for they have been taken for granted by the Democratic Party. The leverage they could assert by a better distribution of their strength between the two great political parties in America has never been fully utilized.

I have tried not to minimize the difficulties facing the Republican Party. I realize the enormous efforts which will be required to overcome our inertia and to infuse Republicanism with the qualities necessary for leadership. I know that the very people who avoid us are precisely the people we need most in order to help us overcome our grave handicaps in popularity and dynamism. But I am fully aware that a welcome may not be extended by party leadership for some time. And because of this, I urge them to force their way into the Republican Party. I urge them to join Republican city, town, ward and precinct committees. I urge them to *participate*. I ask them to intensify their efforts. And I say to them that even though it may not be apparent, the great majority of Republicans in this country welcome them with open arms.

It is no secret that an intense ideological struggle within the Republican Party can probably not be avoided — a struggle which, I trust, will be waged without rancor and bitterness. But the Republican Party is not going to wither away; it is an established American institution with enormous resources for survival. The question is, which direction will it take? Its future, and the future of the country and perhaps the future of the world, hang in the balance. No political activity can have more immediate and direct effect on American and world politics as a whole than participation in the struggle within the Republican Party. For those who yearn to do something constructive for America, to commit themselves to a worthwhile cause and to engage in meaningful political activity, the challenge is clear. I urge the skeptical, the critical, the fearful and the disillusioned to put aside the crutch of noninvolvement and join *this* good fight.

I end this book with high optimism and with a prediction that the Republican Party will soon become the majority party. I believe that there is a great future in store for us. I have faith in our determination to govern. I have faith in our ability to govern. I have faith in the intelligence of the American people to give us the opportunity to govern. And, above all, I have faith in the wisdom and willingness of the Republican Party to respond to the challenge of change so essential if we are to govern.

❖ ❖ ❖

Bibliography

Allen, Frederick Lewis. *Only Yesterday.* New York: Harper, 1931.
Black, Eugene Robert. *The Diplomacy of Economic Development.* Cambridge: Harvard University Press, 1960.
Buckley, William. *Up From Liberalism.* New York: McDowell, Obolensky, 1959.
Burns, James MacGregor. *The Deadlock of Democracy.* Englewood Cliffs, N. J.: Prentice-Hall, 1963.
Clark, Kenneth. *Dark Ghetto.* New York: Harper, 1965.
Commager, Henry Steele and Samuel Eliot Morison. *The Growth of the American Republic.* New York: Oxford Univ. Press, 1962.
Curtis, Francis. *The Republican Party.* New York: Knickerbocker Press, 1904.
Dewey, Thomas E. *The Case Against the New Deal.* New York: Harper, 1940.
Donovan, Robert J. *The Future of the Republican Party.* New York: New American Library, 1964.
Eisenhower, Dwight D. *Waging Peace.* Garden City, N. Y.: Doubleday, 1965.
———. *White House Years: Mandate For Change, 1953-1956.* Garden City, N. Y.: Doubleday, 1963.
Goldwater, Barry M. *Conscience of a Conservative.* New York: McFadden-Bartell, 1964.
———. *Where I Stand.* New York: McGraw-Hill, 1964.
———. *Why Not Victory?* New York: McGraw-Hill, 1962.
Harrington, Michael. *The Other America: Poverty in the U. S.* New York: Macmillan, 1962.
Hearnshaw, F. J. C. *Conservatism in England.* London: Macmillan, 1933.
Hicks, John D. *Republican Ascendancy 1921-1933.* New York: Harper and Row, 1960.
Hoffman, Paul G. *One Hundred Countries, One and One Quarter Billion People: How to Speed Their Economic Growth and Ours in the 1960's.* Washington, D.C.: Albert D. and Mary Lasker Foundation, 1960.
Hofstadter, Richard. *The Age of Reform.* New York: Knopf, 1955.

The Challenge of Change

Humphrey, Hubert. *War on Poverty.* New York: McGraw-Hill, 1964.
Isenberg, Irwin. *The Drive Against Illiteracy.* New York: Wilson, 1964.
Jacobs, Jane. *The Death and Life of Great American Cities.* New York: Random House, 1961.
Javits, Jacob K. *Order of Battle.* New York: Atheneum, 1964.
Johnson, Walter. *1600 Pennsylvania Avenue: Presidents and the People Since 1929.* Boston: Little, Brown, 1963.
Joyner, Conrad. *The Republican Dilemma: Conservatism or Progressivism?* Tucson, Ariz.: Univ. of Arizona Press, 1963.
Key, V. O., Jr. *American Public Opinion and American Democracy.* New York: Knopf, 1964.
———. *Politics, Parties and Pressure Groups.* (4th ed.) New York: Crowell, 1958.
Laird, Melvin R., ed. *The Conservative Papers.* Chicago: Quadrangle, 1964.
Larson, Arthur. *A Republican Looks at His Party.* New York: Harper, 1956.
Link, Arthur S. *Woodrow Wilson and the Progressive Era.* New York: Harper, 1954.
Lippmann, Walter. *Conversations with Walter Lippmann.* Boston: Little, Brown, 1965.
———. *The Good Society.* Boston: Little, Brown, 1937.
Lubell, Samuel. *Future of American Politics.* New York: Harper, 1952.
———. *The Revolt of the Moderates.* New York: Harper, 1956.
Marshall, Burke. *Federalism and Civil Rights.* New York: Columbia Univ. Press, 1964.
Mayer, George. *The Republican Party.* New York: Oxford Univ. Press, 1964.
Mendelson, Wallace. *Discrimination.* Englewood Cliffs, N. J.: Prentice-Hall, 1962.
Miller, Herman P. *Rich Man, Poor Man.* New York: Crowell, 1964.
Moley, Raymond. *The Republican Opportunity.* New York: Duell, Sloan & Pearce, 1962.
———. *The Republican Opportunity in 1964.* New York: Duell, Sloan & Pearce, 1964.
Moos, Malcom. *The Republicans: A History of Their Party.* New York: Random House, 1956.
Morgenthau, Hans J. *The Crossroad Papers: A Look into the American Future.* New York: Norton, 1965.
Myrdal, Gunnar. *Challenge to Affluence.* New York: Pantheon, 1963.
Novak, Robert D. *The Agony of the GOP, 1964.* New York: Macmillan, 1965.
Paddock, Paul and William Paddock. *Hungry Nations.* Boston: Little, Brown, 1964.
President's Commission on National Goals. *Goals for Americans.* Englewood Cliffs, N. J.: Prentice-Hall, 1960.

Bibliography

Rauch, Basil. *The History of the New Deal.* New York: Creative Age Press, Inc., 1944.

Ripon Society. *Election '64: A Ripon Society Report.* January, 1965. Cambridge, Mass.

Rockefeller, Nelson A. *The Future of Federalism.* Cambridge, Mass.: Harvard Univ. Press, 1962.

Roosevelt, James, ed. *The Liberal Papers.* Garden City, N. Y.: Doubleday, Anchor paperback.

Ross, J. F. Hoffman and Paul Levack, eds. *Burke's Politics — Selected Writings and Speeches of Edmund Burke.* New York: Knopf, 1949.

Rossi, Petter Henry. *The Politics of Urban Renewal: The Chicago Findings.* Glencoe, Ill.: Free Press, 1961.

Rossiter, Clinton. *Conservatism in America.* New York: Knopf, 1955.

——. *Parties and Politics in America.* Ithaca, N. Y.: Cornell Univ. Press, 1964.

Saveth, Edward N. *Understanding the American Past.* Boston: Little, Brown, 1954.

Schlesinger, Arthur M., Jr. *The Age of Jackson.* Boston: Little, Brown, 1945.

——. *The Coming of the New Deal.* Vol. 2. Boston: Houghton Mifflin, 1958.

——. *Crisis of the Old Order.* Boston: Houghton Mifflin, 1957.

——. *The Vital Center.* Boston: Houghton Mifflin, 1949.

Sexton, Patricia C. *Spanish Harlem.* New York: Harper and Row, 1965.

Smith, T. V. and Robert A. Taft. *Foundations of Democracy.* New York: Columbia Univ. Press, 1939.

Stevenson, Adlai E. *Call to Greatness.* New York: Harper, 1954.

Stromberg, Roland N. *Republicanism Reappraised.* Washington, D. C.: Public Affairs Press, 1952.

Taft, Robert A. *A Foreign Policy for Americans.* Garden City, N. Y.: Doubleday, 1951.

Viereck, Peter. *Conservatism from John Adams to Churchill.* New York: D. Van Nostrand, Inc., 1956.

——. *Conservatism Revisited.* New York: Scribner's, 1949.

Ward, Barbara. *The Rich Nations and the Poor Nations.* New York: Norton, 1962.

White, R. J. *The Conservative Tradition.* New York: New York Univ. Press, 1957.

White, Theodore H. *The Making of the President, 1960.* New York: Atheneum, 1961.

——. *The Making of the President, 1964.* New York: Atheneum, 1965.

White, William S. *The Taft Story.* New York: Harper, 1954.

Willkie, Wendell. *One World.* New York: Simon and Schuster, 1943.

Zinn, Howard. *SNCC: The New Abolitionists.* Boston: Beacon Press, 1964.

✤ ✤ ✤

Biographical Note

EDWARD W. BROOKE was born in Washington, D.C., on October 26, 1919. After graduating from Howard University in 1941 and after his service as an army officer in the Second World War, he entered Boston University Law School, where he was editor of the *Boston University Law Review* and received his LL.B. in 1948 and his LL.M. in 1950. Mr. Brooke holds honorary degrees from several universities, among them Northeastern University, American International College, and Worcester Polytechnic Institute.

Currently, Mr. Brooke is Attorney General of the Commonwealth of Massachusetts, the highest elected Negro official in the nation. He is a Fellow of the American Bar Association, a Trustee of Boston University, a Fellow of the American Academy of Arts and Sciences, President of The Opera Company of Boston, Inc., and serves as well in many other capacities outside his position as Attorney General.

The Challenge of Change is his first book.